Archaeological Investigations
at Molpa, San Diego County, California

Archaeological Investigations at Molpa, San Diego County, California

By

D. L. TRUE, C. W. MEIGHAN, AND HARVEY CREW

with appendix by Smiley Karst

UNIVERSITY OF CALIFORNIA PRESS

BERKELEY · LOS ANGELES · LONDON

University of California Publications in Anthropology

Volume 11

Approved for publication January 12, 1973

University of California Press
Berkeley and Los Angeles, California

University of California Press, Ltd.
London, England

isbn: 0-520-09490-5

Library of Congress Catalog Card Number: 73-620021

CONTENTS

1. PROBLEMS AND METHODS

This report describes and interprets the finds at Molpa, a historically known Luiseño village on the slopes of Mount Palomar in San Diego County, California (see map 1; pl. 1). Molpa is important as the type site used to define the nature of a protohistoric archaeological complex or assembalge occurring widely in the San Luis Rey River drainage. Our account provides one step toward development of a clearer and more precise definition of the late, pottery-using horizon of southern California archaeology, a widespread series of assemblages with considerable variety of archaeological manifestations.

Because of the diversity of its geography and aboriginal cultures, California archaeology in general lacks assemblages of wide spatial distribution and fairly consistent content. The result has been a proliferation of cultural or assemblage names, arrived at by various sorts of investigations and often poorly defined, particularly in southern California. In 1959, Meighan identified more than one hundred names of archaeological cultures for the state of California (Meighan 1959b: fig. 6), and more such terms have been added since. Figs. 1 through 3 show the present terminology and time placement of southern California archaeological assemblages.

Names of archaeological complexes in California have been derived from two kinds of investigations. Some terms, such as "Yuman" used by M. J. Rogers (1945) arose from broad surveys of extensive areas but lacked detailed site reports. At the other extreme, names of complexes have been set up from carefully controlled excavations of sites considered typical (such as the Sayles Complex, Kowta 1969) or the San Luis Rey I assemblage (Meighan 1954); in such cases the exact areal extent of the complex may be poorly known because of inadequate studies in the surrounding area.

It is obvious that both site reports and areal

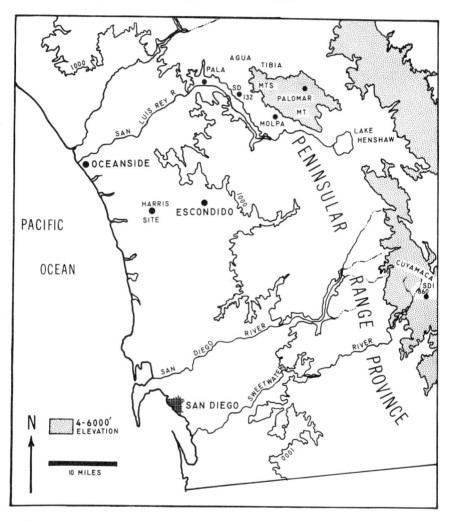

Map 1. Western San Diego County and general area discussed in Molpa report.

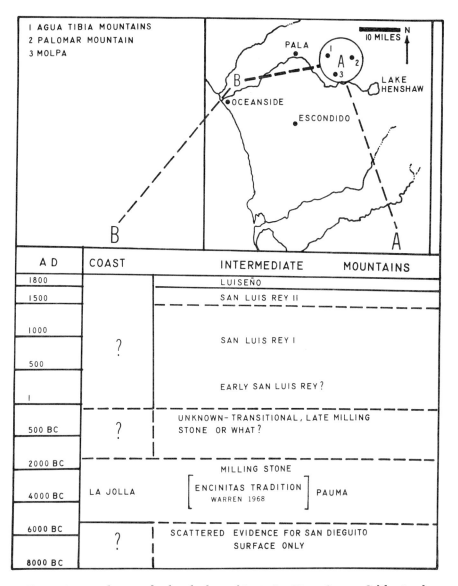

Fig. 1. Suggested time and cultural relationships in San Diego County, California, along a transect extending from the Palomar Mountain region to the coast near the city of Oceanside. This is all within the territory designated as San Luis Rey.

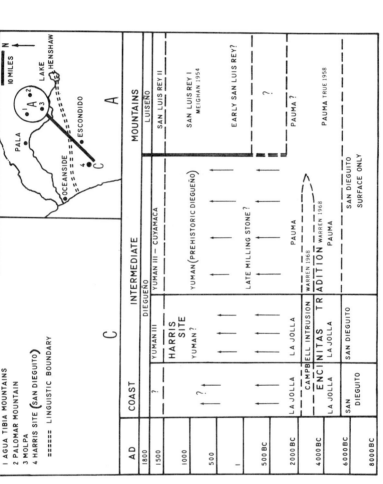

Fig. 2. Suggested time and cultural relationships in San Diego County, California, along a transect extending from the Palomar Mountain region to the coastal plain south and west of the city of Escondido. This transect includes territory belonging to both the Luiseño (San Luis Rey) and the Diegueño (Cuyamaca) peoples.

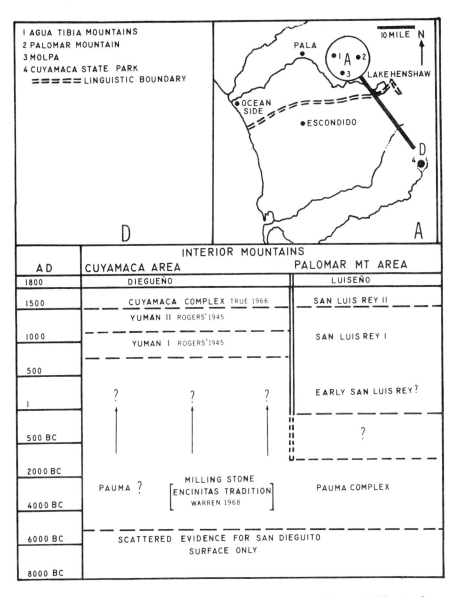

Fig. 3. Suggested time and cultural relationships in San Diego County, California, along a transect extending from Palomar Mountain region to the Laguna Mountain region in the vicinity of Cuyamaca Rancho State Park. This transect includes territory of the San Luis Rey and Cuyamaca complexes.

surveys are necessary to define properly an archaeological complex. It is, however, essential that there be at least one carefully described site where excavation has provided a reasonably large sample to show the nature and content of the archaeological complex. The site of Molpa serves that need for the complex labeled San Luis Rey II, and the data provided here should eliminate much archaeological argument about what is or is not a part of the San Luis Rey complex, as well as show the similarities and differences between San Luis Rey II and other late culture variants in southern California.

The importance of a type site and a descriptive site report to be used in conjunction with detailed surveys and intensive evaluation of archaeological resources recovered from all sites in the area can be clearly demonstrated in the confusion surrounding all of the pottery-using late prehistoric cultures of southern California. Efforts in southern California archaeology have been concentrated on the earlier assemblages with the result that we know far more about the archaeological remains of several thousand years ago than about the more recent sites. Work has also been concentrated on the coast so that we have many reports for coastal sites, but very few for sites even a few miles inland. Considering these lacks, the careful description of the Molpa excavation is of general value to all chronological and comparative studies in southern California.

Our first problem, therefore, was a descriptive one, assembling and defining the characteristics of an archaeological culture known to exist but not yet defined from excavation data. In Chapter 2 the definition of the San Luis Rey complex is set forth as revealed by the Molpa excavation.

The methods for excavation were standard and involved no innovations. The location of the excavations was largely dictated by the presence of granite outcrops over much of the site; these also had an effect on aboriginal activities, so that our digging corresponds to a considerable extent to the activity areas of the aboriginal peoples even though we did not design the excavation with this in mind.

   With the San Luis Rey II materials defined from our
sample we then faced two additional problems of more
analytical nature. The first is the comparison and contrasting of San Luis Rey II with adjacent cultures in
time and space, as discussed in Chapter 3. Such comparative study is commonly presented in archaeological
site reports, but we made an effort to go beyond the
listing of trait similarities and evaluate what the
similarities and differences may have meant culturally.
This is a central problem for archaeologists — what do
we mean when we say that two assemblages are "alike" or
"different"? We may ignore the matter, merely presenting lists of shared elements. Or we may choose, con-
sciously or unconsciously, to stress the similarities,
an approach which leads, in an area of hunter-gatherers
at least, to a somewhat misleading impression of uni-
formity among the prehistoric cultures. Conversely, we
may follow the common practice of stressing the unique-
ness of descriptive details, so that minor stylistic
variations in such things as projectile points are
given the status of separate cultures, peoples, or
tribes.
   These biases have little effect when one compares
assemblages of major difference, such as agricultural
versus hunter-gather sites. But within a region like
southern California, which remained on a hunter-gatherer
level until historic times, the conclusions to be drawn
from the archaeology are greatly altered by how the
archaeologist conceptualizes his archaeological evidence as being like or unlike comparable remains. We
have therefore made a conscious effort to evaluate
similarities and differences between San Luis Rey II
and adjacent assemblages. For example, in preliminary
reports it was said that San Luis Rey II was no more
than San Luis Rey I plus pottery. We discuss in some
detail whether this is true, and if it is true what it
may mean culturally. While our efforts to deal with
the problem of comparisons must be regarded as limited
and only partly successful, we feel that they are a
step forward in dealing with a central and universal
archaeological concern.
   A final set of problems, discussed in Chapter 4,
came to our attention in attempting interpretation

of the Molpa collection. The California archaeologist
is blessed with the fact that the nineteenth-century
Indians of the state were the direct descendents of
many of the Indians recovered archaeologically, living
lives not unlike those of their ancestors. This,
coupled with abundant and detailed ethnographic information collected by early ethnographers, particularly
A. L. Kroeber and his students beginning about 1900,
allows the archaeologist to flesh out the scanty archaeological collections with ethnohistorical information.
For Molpa itself, since the site extends into the
historic period we were able to make use of ethnohistory from Luiseño, Diegueño, and other southern
California groups. Data utilized here were derived
from the published literature as indicated above, and
from intensive work with surviving Luiseño some of whom
were able to refer directly to Molpa and its artifacts.

The ethnohistorical information from these sources
provides us with a fair amount of data on artifact func-
tions, ritual use of objects, and the nature of religious structures and ceremonies, all of which allows
valuable insights into the possibilities and realities
of archaeological interpretations. Applying the ethnohistoric data as a check on the kinds of interpretations
the archaeologist would make if he had only his archaeological collection as evidence, we come to two
conclusions. The first is a reinforcement of archaeological caution and a recognition of how great are the
limitations of interpretation from archaeological data
alone. Particularly for the remains of hunter-gatherers,
it is evident that the archaeologist can make plausible
but erroneous interpretations, and that his verifiable
interpretations must be disappointingly limited unless
he has ethnohistoric data, or at the least a strong
ethnographic analogy, to back up his statements about
artifact use and meaning.

The ethnohistoric observations in this context also
allow us to evaluate the theoretical position of many
contemporary archaeologists, particularly the stress
laid on man's "adaptive" responses, and the feeling
that archaeological remains always reflect laws of ecological adaptation. The Molpa data make clear the

difficulty of using such a theoretical position to interpret specific sites and assemblages, and especially underline the difficulty inherent in attempts to extend the interpretation of archaeologically recovered material culture remains into the realm of social organization and other ideational aspects of prehistoric cultures.

In presenting our findings, we have coped with the ever present dilemma of the modern archaeologist. On the one hand, he may be criticized for presenting tedious details of insignificant artifacts — a mere catalog of relics with little effort at understanding. At the opposite extreme, it is possible to be so theoretical that complex methodologies are applied along with unprovable assumptions, yielding conclusions that go far beyond the realities of the evidence. Our archaeological field study is like most others in being a compromise between these two extremes — an effort to avoid armchair theorizing and yet use the archaeological facts to some intellectual purpose.

2. EXCAVATION OF MOLPA AND DESCRIPTION OF THE SAN LUIS REY II ASSEMBLAGE

BACKGROUND

In the decade from 1951 to 1961 a number of archaeological projects were initiated in San Diego County, California, by the Department of Anthropology, University of California, Los Angeles. These included numerous surveys as well as limited excavations on several sites (Eberhart 1952 unpublished ms; Meighan 1954, 1959a; True 1954; 1957, 1958; True and Meighan 1959 and appendix A this volume; Warren and True 1961; Warren, True and Eudey 1961).

Based on data gained from the earlier of these works, Meighan (1954) defined the San Luis Rey Complex and recognized in this complex two phases or subphases for the late prehistoric and protohistoric period in San Diego County (San Luis Rey I and San Luis Rey II). The earlier nonceramic phase (SLR I) was defined on the basis of the excavations at SD-132 (Meighan 1954). The pottery-bearing phase described in the same report was defined on the basis of surface collections, of ethnographic accounts, and of published reports from other parts of San Diego County. At that time, then, only the SLR-I phase was defined specifically on the basis of an excavated sample from the designated area (northern San Diego County). The existence of a pottery-bearing phase was recognized, but its exact artifact inventory and spatial boundaries had not yet been defined. Data from excavated sites used to support a San Luis Rey II phase were limited to one inadequate typescript report (Mc Cown 1948) for northern San Diego County, and several short reports on work in the southern part of the county (Mc Cown 1945; Treganza 1942; Rogers 1945).

At the time, this information from the southern county was considered pertinent to the definition of the San Luis Rey II phase in the northern part of the county. However, to emphasize the distinct character of San Luis Rey II in relation to the more broadly defined concept of Yuman III as the latter was defined

by M. J. Rogers (1945), it was deemed necessary to excavate at least one pottery-bearing site <u>within</u> the San
Luis Rey Basin, apart from those sites believed to be
more typical of the Yuman III pattern.

With this in mind excavations were initiated in
1955 at a protohistoric site known to the Luiseño as
Molpa (SDi-308). This location was well within the
territory believed to belong to the San Luis Rey; it
was a pottery-bearing site, and it had the potential for
considerable midden depth and thus a possible stratigraphic demonstration of the relative position of the
two proposed San Luis Rey phases.

Excavations at SDi-308 were carried out intermit-
tently from 1955 through 1957 by field classes in archaeology from the University of California, Los
Angeles. The work was under the direction of C. W.
Meighan, assisted by William Harrison.

As with any attempt to work up material twelve or
more years after it was excavated, our effort must,
in many respects, be considered a compromise. It is intended as a descriptive statement with an emphasis upon
the artifact inventory believed to be typical of the
late prehistoric-protohistoric period in this region.
In the course of the present study all of the artifacts
were re-examined and recorded on edge-punched cards for
future reference. The site was remapped and studied
with respect to topography and features. Artifact provenience, pit profiles, and excavated features, however,
are described on the basis of the original field records
and notes.

Because of the time span since the excavations were
completed, and because some of the original finds and
records have been incorporated into museum middens and
could not be located, we cannot suggest that the results presented here represent a standard for modern
archaeological reporting. However, in view of the small
amount of material availble from this part of southern
California for this period of time, it was felt that
even a compromise effort would be justifiable and
useful.

THE SETTING

In north-central San Diego County the Peninsular
Range Province is dominated by the Agua Tibia Mountains.
This range, with elevations in places of more than 6,000
feet, is best known perhaps as the platform supporting
the 200-inch Hale telescope on Palomar Mountain, the
mountain itself forming the southernmost anchor of the
Agua Tibias (see map 1). Physiographically and struc-
turally this range consists of an uplifted series of
granitic batholiths. It appears to be a horst und
graben type feature with the southwestern face delin-
eated by the main Elsinore fault zone and the northeastern scarp marked by what is probably a branch of
the same system (for references supporting these data
see Larsen 1948, 1951; Mann 1955; Ellis and Lee 1919).

Along the southwestern flank of Palomar Mountain
at an elevation of about 2,800 feet, the scarp is broken by a series of flats that mark the location of the
Elsinore fault zone. At this point, the fault trends
southeast to northwest from the Valle de Jose region
(presently occupied by Lake Henshaw) toward the town of
Pala near the northwestern end of the main Agua Tibia
range.

This particular structural configuration is of
concern here because many of the prehistoric settlements in the area are concentrated on the flats marking
the fault zone (see pl. 1). Springs usually associated
with a faulted topography provide water sources for
several of these settlements including that of Molpa.

Vegetation on the flats differs somewhat from that
of the adjacent terrain and is essentially oak parkland
(savannah). Because of the differences in elevation,
exposure, and parent rock, the terrain adjacent to the
oak parkland regions supports a wide variety of vegetation. The steeper mountain sides and canyons along the
southwestern boundary of the fault zone support a typical southern California chaparral. The flanks of
Palomar Mountain above the flats support chaparral on
the lower slopes and mixed broadleaf coniferous forests
higher on the mountain. Small flats or benches on the
mountain flanks are marked by oak groves. The canyons
themselves contain gallery forest, oak groves and some

conifers as low as 3,000 feet elevation in favored
locations.

Relatively high orographic precipitation along the
southwestern rim of the mountain proper (up to 50
inches per year) supports a dense and quite lush mixed
broadleaf and coniferous forest environment at an elevation of some 5,000 feet. This contrasts with rain-
fall in the lower elevations of less than 15 inches
per year.

The wide range of vegetation extending through
several environmental zones plus localized environmental conditions provided a broad and generally rich subsistence base for the prehistoric inhabitants of the
area. Table 1 lists some of the more common plants
found in this region. A substantial portion of this
inventory contributed in one way or another to the
aboriginal subsistence.

This vegetation, in addition to its direct contri-
bution to aboriginal subsistence, also supported assorted
fauna which in turn were exploited by the Indian inhabitants. Except for localized adjustments in response to
short term wet and dry cycles there is no evidence that
conditions here have altered much over the past 500 to
800 years.

THE SITE

Molpa (SDi-308) is located within the Boucher Hill
Quadrangle (USGS 7 1/2 minutes series) at an elevation
of 2,500 feet in northern San Diego County, California
(see maps 1 and 2; pl. 1).

The settlement covered portions of two low knolls
along the edge of a low ridge, overlooking an open grass-
land area formed in part by fault controlled slumping.
A small but reliable spring is located at the base of
the slope below the site. The site is marked by conspicuous granitic bedrock exposures. The entire area
seems to be covered with a well-developed midden although there is considerable variation in the depth of
the deposit. The midden covers some 40,000 square
yards; some if it may represent outwash from the higher
slopes (see pls. 2 and 3 for views on the site proper).

TABLE 1

Common Plants Found in the Territory
Exploited by the Villages of Molpa and Cuca
(See map 1)

Chaparral —exposed slopes and hillsides: Only the more
common genera are listed. The composition of this
community varies from locale to locale.

Plant	Luiseño name	Use (where known)
Adenostoma fasiculatum	ʔuʔu t	tools, gum
Eriogonum fasciculatum	wulaqla	medicine
Quercus dumosa	pa wis	food, medicine
Quercus chrysolepis	wiʔat	food and games
Garrya flavescens	not known	not stated
Ceanothus leucodermis	ʔuʔu sawat	not stated
Arctostaphylos species	ko lul	food
Zylococcus bicolor	not known	food (?)

Canyons and areas marginal to heavy stands of chaparral:
Often better watered and have more favorable soils than
the slopes above. Includes small flats and benches
adjacent to streams.

Quercus agrifolia	wiʔa sal	food
Quercus wislizeni	not known	food
Quercus engelmanni	to vasal	food and gum
Photinia arbutifolia	ʔa cawut	food
Prunas ilicifolia	ca mis	food

(14)

TABLE 1 (continued)

Plant	Luiseño name	Use (where known)
Rhus laurina	naqwut	food (?)
Rhus ovata	pa naqwut	food (drinks)
Rhus trilobata	so val	baskets, food, religion, medicine
Rhus integrifolia	not known	food (drinks)
Rhus diversiloba	ɂiya l	poison oak (use?)
Turricola parryi	ɂato vaykat	medicine, pottery
Salvia apiana	qa sil	food, medicine, religion
Salvia munzii (mellifera)	qa navut	food (?)
Salvia carduacea	pa lit	food, medicine
Salvia columbariae	pa sal	food, medicine
Sambucus coerulea	ku tpat	tools, medicine, food, religion
Artemisia dracunucula	wa cis	medicine
Lupinus longifolius	not known	food (?)
Pickeringia montana	not known	food (?)
Lotus scoparius	ki wat	?
Solanum xanti (species?)	takavsis	dye, medicine, possible food

(15)

TABLE 1 (continued)

Plant	Luiseño name	Use (where known)
Datura meteloides	nagtumus	religion
Mimulus species	not known	?
Penstemon anterrhinoides	sexla and pi mal	?
Baccharis douglasii (?)	morwaxpis	tools, medicine
Ephedra species (Californica)	not known	drink, medicine (?)
Epicampes rigens	yulalas	basket foundation
Echinocystis macrocarpa	ʔenwis	medicine, games paint base
Yucca whipplei	pana l	food
Yucca mohavensis	hunu vat	food, fiber
Opuntia species	na vut	food, tools

Gallery forest: Wet locations along streams considerable overlap with species listed above.

Populus fremontii (cottonwood)	ʔaˀva xat	?
Salix species	wat Saxa naxat	?
Salix lasiolepsis	saxat	tools
Quercus species (Sycamore)	sive la	?

(16)

TABLE 1 (continued)

Plant	Luiseño name	Use (where known)
Sambucus species	not known	food, etc.
Rosa californica	ɔusla	medicine, gum, religion
Rhus diversiloba	Piya l	poison oak(use?)
Rubus vitifolius	Pikwla	food, dye (?)
Vitis girdiana	makwit	food
Urtica gracilis	sakisla	religion, fiber medicine
Scirpus microcarpus	pacxayal	tools, religion, basket-making, mats, food?
Juncus acutus	soyla	basket-making, mats, food?
Montia perfoliata	not known	food

Mountain regions: Locally above 4,000 foot elevation usually near 5,000 in this area.

Pinus species	pawxit	?
Pinus coulteri	wixenivisla	
Librocedrus decurrens	tuvot	shelter(?)
Pseudotsuga macrocarpa	yuyla	?
Abies concolor	ɔuɔu mal	?
Quercus kellogii	kwi la	food
Quercus chrysolepis	wiɔat	food

(17)

TABLE 1 (continued)

Plant	Luiseño name	Use (where known)
Quercus englemanni	to vasal	food
Prunus virginiana (demissa)	ʔaʔtut	food
Berberis pinnata	not known	food(?)
Ribes nevadense	not known	food
Ribes speciosum	wusocis	food
Rosa woodsii	not known	?
Rhamnus crocea	not known	food(?)
Rhamnus californica	not known	medicine(?)
Rhamnus purshiana (buckthorn)	not known	medicine

Other plants from the general locality.

Brodiaea pulchella	to kapis	food, religion
Chenopodium californicum	qaxa wut	food, soap
Asclepias eriocarpa	tokmat	fiber, gum
Trifolium gracilentum	queʔquis	food
Bloomeria species	qawicxal	food, religion
Euphrobia polycarpa	qenxamal	medicine
Anemopsis californica	cevnis	medicine

(18)

TABLE 1 (continued)

Plant	Luiseno name	Use (where known)
Psoralea macrostachya	piʔmukvul	fiber, medicine, dye, religion, thatching
Croton californicus var.	suʔi kawut	medicine
Centaurium venustum	zasoskit	medicine
Cucurbita foetidissima	ne xis	soap

This list is not intended to be complete and there are hundreds more species of plants within the area. It does indicate the range of material, and the nature of the plant utilization by the Luiseno. The Luiseño names and uses of these plants were provided by Max Peters, Herman Calac, and Henry Rodriquez. The Luiseño terminology was checked and corrected by William Bright, Department of Anthropology, University of California, Los Angeles.

Seventeen excavation units and one strata trench were excavated (see map 3 and fig. 4; pl. 2 indicates location of Trench J). The units were 5-foot-by-5-foot squares and were excavated in arbitrary 6-inch levels. The midden was removed with trowels and shovels, and all of it was sifted through 1/4-inch mesh screen. Trowels were used for all detailed excavation and all features were exposed and pedestaled for examination and recording; 45.8 cubic yards of midden were examined in this manner. Eight-hundred and eighty-six artifacts were recovered, not including potsherds. In addition to the primary excavation area, exploration was carried out in the northwest portion of the larger site area along the margins of the site proper. Here a test trench about 2 feet wide and 50 feet long was excavated in an east-west direction to look for a possible cemetary location (map 3). Because of the irregular depth of the midden the total volume for the site is not known, but the excavation sample is estimated to comprise about 3 to 5 percent of the midden.

In the excavation on site (Trench J and Trench A) the midden ranged from 60 inches in Pit J-21 to less than 12 inches in J-36. In many locations marginal to the bedrock exposures the cultural deposit is less than 6 inches deep. Throughout the main site area the midden examined was loose, friable, and ashy, typical of late site deposits in southern California upland areas.

The soil deposit at the marginal test trench differs markedly from the midden. It is higher in clay content, lacks the ashy characteristic, and is devoid of organic refuse and faunal remains. The test trench location is clearly not part of the main occupation area.

The basic soil of the immediate area surrounding the site itself is a thin, poorly developed residual clay loam developing over a gruess base. In some locations there is some redeposition caused by sheet erosion and down-slope movement. The surface of the open flat area below the site is in part made up of redeposited clay soils, and in part consists of alluvial deposits resulting from stream flows draining the mountain itself. The midden appears to be a mixture of the clay loam base modified by organic supplements and burning. It tends to have a sandy texture and no doubt includes some sorted outwash from the higher slopes. No obvious stratification was noted within this deposit, and except for artifact differences it is homogeneous from top to bottom. The artifactual material under discussion here represents a sample from only a small portion of the total site area. It is considered likely that it is a representative sample of the latest phase of the site occupation, but neither the excavated artifacts nor the features discovered in the course of the excavations can tell us much about the nature and distribution of activities within the site. This kind of analysis calls for sampling over a much wider area within the site and for a much larger sample than is presently available. The bedrock milling stones, of course, are obvious indications of food preparation activities and probably represent women's work areas (see figures A-8 and pl. 4). Also we can suggest that any houses or structures would have been located within the three or four small relatively flat areas on the site (pls. 2 and 3). At least two pictograph rocks are included within the site and a possible ceremonial area is suggested by the presence of a pitted boulder in a central location within the site (figure 6 and pl. 5). Thus we are able to suggest activity areas based on site features, but cannot relate these activities to specific tools in any statistical sense.

Based primarily on the distribution of potsherds in the main deposit and typical milling-stone elements recovered from the test trench area, it is suggested that three separate components are represented in the deposits at Molpa:

1. Pauma complex occupation —An interior upland manifestation of a milling-stone horizon probably related in some way with the coastal La Jolla milling-stone complex or culture (True 1958; Warren, True and Eudey 1961; Shumway, Hubbs, and Moriarty, 1961; Warren 1964). Evidence of a milling-stone occupation was limited to a few artifacts from the test trench area (see figs. 1-3 and map 3).

2. San Luis Rey I occupation— This phase is represented by the lower levels of the midden on

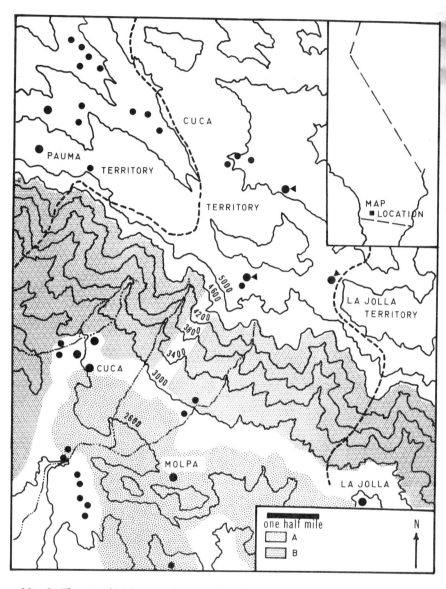

Map 2. The site of Molpa in relation to the villages of Cuca and La Jolla. Shaded area A indicates the general boundaries of the oak parkland (savannah) vegetation. Shaded area B represents the approximate boundaries of the steep hillside and canyon chaparral communities. The unshaded territory *above* 4,600 foot elevation represents mixed broadleaf and coniferous forest. The heavy dashed lines mark the approximate boundaries of the Cuca/Molpa territory on the mountain. Archaeological sites are indicated by black circles. Important summer camps belonging to the villages of Cuca and Molpa are further marked with a black triangle.

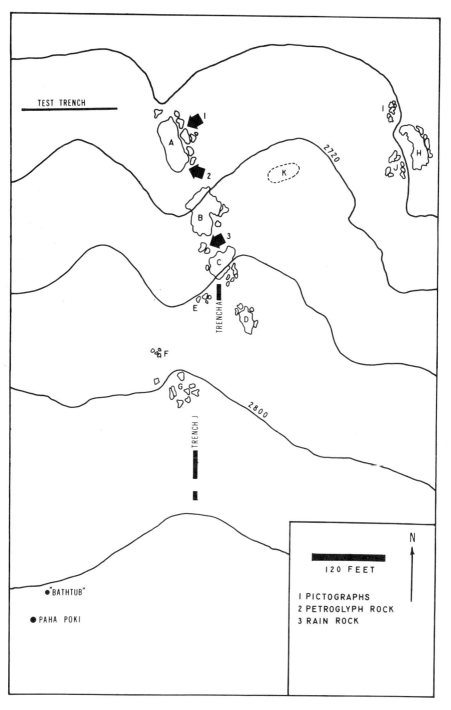

TEST TRENCH

TRENCH A

TRENCH J

•"BATHTUB"

•PAHA POKI

120 FEET

N

1 PICTOGRAPHS
2 PETROGLYPH ROCK
3 RAIN ROCK

Map 3. Location of major features and excavated areas at site SDi–308 (Molpa).

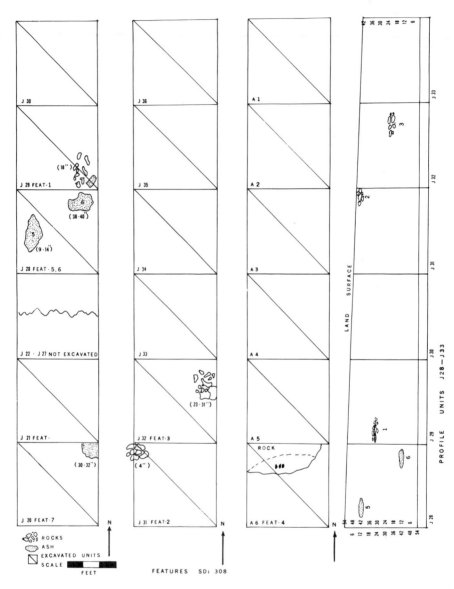

Fig. 4. Excavated units and subsurface features at Molpa (see also map 2).

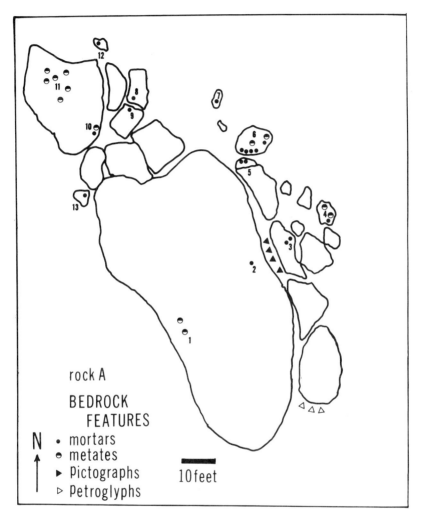

Fig. 5. Location of surface features relative to outcroppings of Rock A. (See map 2 for location of Rock A on the site proper.)

the site proper. Those levels deeper than 30 inches are classified as SLR-I. However, there may be places within the site where SLR-I material can be found at a lesser depth. It is unlikely that all of the site area was occupied at the same time so that there may be locations within the site that actually represent SLR-I occupation, with little or no overlying SLR-II occupation. The problem is that the preceramic or nonceramic assemblages are masked by the mixing that took place during the latest period of occupation. A large number of Luiseño ritual activities involved the digging of pits and various other modifications of the site surface. This plus normal living activities over several hundred years would be likely to mix potsherds into a great deal of the exposed upper surface of the midden. However, the assemblages taken from the lower levels tend to duplicate the material described in the SLR-I type site report (Meighan 1954: 223).

For the purpose of this report we omit description of the material recovered from the test trench area (Pauma Complex). In addition, the limited number of units penetrating the SLR-I component and the relatively small sample recovered from these units makes it difficult to say more about San Luis Rey I than has been already published. The emphasis here is therefore directed toward the San Luis Rey II component. San Luis Rey I artifacts are included in the analysis and description but the majority of the collection is reprisentative of the latest period of occupation rather than the earliest.

FEATURES

Features at Molpa are considered here in two categories: (1) those uncovered in the course of the excavations, and (2) those surface features found on the site as bedrock mortars and millingstones, and pictograph/petroglyph locations.

Excavated Features

The field records indicate that seven subsurface features were encountered in the course of the 1955-1956 excavations. The location of the excavated trenches is indicated on map 3. The location of the features in the units is plotted on figure 4. For the most part these consist of small rock cairns or clusters, and ash concentrations believed to have been fire places. The size of the excavated sample and the discontinuous nature of the exposed areas makes it difficult to assess the significance of these features in terms of specific activities.

Feature 1 (J-29, 18-21 inches depth)

An area approximately 41 by 27 inches in the southeast corner of Pit J-29 contained a greater than normal concentration of rock cobbles and fragments as well as scattered bits of ash. A more concentrated ash lens was located in the extreme southeast corner of the unit. This lends was 12 inches wide, 14 inches long, and 3 inches deep. The possibility of an associated floor was investigated with no confirmation. No artifacts were recorded with this feature.

Feature 2 (J-31, 0-4 inches depth)

A small rock concentration of undetermined significance. At least some of the rock fragments were burned. Two milling-stone fragments were associated. Part of the feature extended into unit K-31.

Feature 3 (J-32, 22-30 inches depth)

A rock concentration in the northeast corner of the pit. The size of this feature is not known. One mano-pestle combination and two mortar fragments were associated. Three of the stones are recorded as "worked" but we have no details.

Feature 4 (A-6)

An artifact cache under the edge of a boulder. Included were one mano, one mano-pestle combination, and
one steatite shaft straightener.

Feature 5 (J-28, 9-14 inches depth)

A concentration of white ash 9 by 17 inches and
approximately 5 inches thick. No artifacts were associated with the feature.

Feature 6 (J-28, 38-40 inches deptn)

A concentration of white ash, 15 inches in diameter and 2 inches deep.

Feature 7 (J-20, 30-32 inches depth)

An ash concentration 10 by 12 inches in dimension
and 2 inches thick. It extended into adjacent units
which were not excavated.

Bedrock Milling Features

A large portion of the entire site area is covered
with bedrock exposures. A substantial number of these
contain mortars and milling-stone features of one kind
or another. Five kinds of bedrock milling or grinding
elements were recorded:
1. Slicks — smooth polished surfaces with no obvious
   depression.
2. Shallow milling surfaces (metates); both oval and
   round forms are present. The cultural or functional differences of the two forms are not known.
   Since there is no obvious patterning to the dis-
   tributions, the differences here may be due to the
   nature of the bedrock and use rather than to differences in time or the peoples responsible for
   them.
3. Shallow bedrock mortars — probably the bases for

basket mortars. They are not deep enough for seed grinding without a basket hopper.
4. Deep bedrock mortars with both round and slightly oval forms. The oval configuration is probably the result of use and parent rock characteristics rather than intent on the part of the makers.
5. Combinations— mortars within slicks or shallow milling areas and mortars with small "pockets" or metate-like areas adjacent to the mortar hole.

The location of each of the major outcrops within the site proper is indicated on map 3. The number and kind of elements recorded for each of these outcrops is presented in table 2. Dimensional data are included in table 3. (Plate 4 illustrates some typical mortar combinations at Molpa.)

The area designated "K" on map 3 is the upper portion of a large expanse of bedrock along the northern margin of the site proper. Most of this outcrop does not contain any evidence of milling activities. The upper edge, however, does contain an unknown number of mortars and possibly other kinds of milling elements. Because this portion of the outcrop has been covered with silt and a thicket of cactus (Opuntia), no attempt was made to map the distribution of the features. Several man-days would be required to clear the area.

In addition to those elements not recorded in area "K", there are other scattered boulders and outcrops around the margins of the site— mostly outside of the midden deposit— that also contain an occasional mortar or milling element. Some of these have been covered with silt or vegetation and others are weathered, suggesting that some elements may be older than those in the central part of the site. Because it is obvious that we have not mapped or recorded all bedrock milling-stone features for the larger area, it is important to recognize that the figures presented in table 2 cannot be used in any strictly controlled comparisons or analyses. The count does include the majority of the elements and is indicative of the relative size or complexity of the site, but probably is meaningless for any statistically based study.

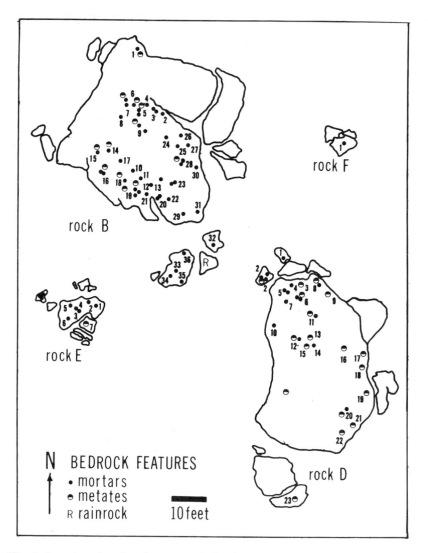

Fig. 6. Location of surface features on bedrock outcroppings B, D, E and F. This includes the rainrock feature. (See map 2 for location of these outcroppings within the site.)

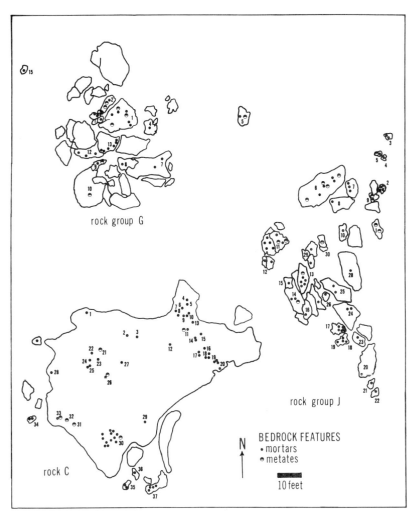

Fig. 7. Location of surface features on bedrock outcroppings C, G, and J. (See map 2 for location of these rock groups within the site.)

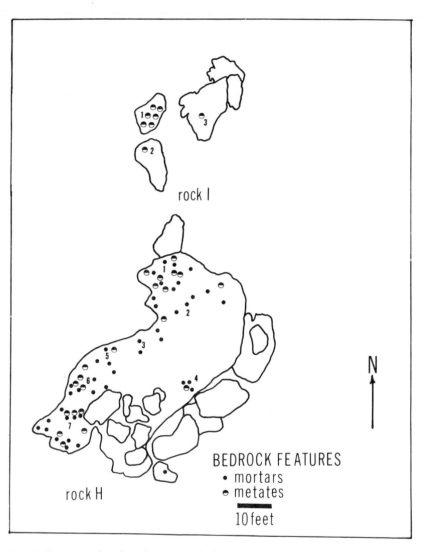

rock I

BEDROCK FEATURES
• mortars
◦ metates

10 feet

rock H

Fig. 8. Location of surface features on bedrock outcroppings H and I. (See map 2 for location of these rock groups within the site.)

TABLE 2

Distribution of Milling Stones and Mortars at Molpa

	Mortars	Milling Areas	Combinations
Rock group A (figure 2)	19	14	Two milling areas with superimposed mortars(3)
Rock group B (figure 3)	48	12	Nine milling areas with superimposed mortars(18)
Rock group C (figure 4)	58	12	Two milling areas with superimposed mortars(2)
Rock group D (figure 3)	16	18	Four milling areas with superimposed mortars(5)
Rock group E (figure 3)	9	1	None
Rock group F (figure 3)	1	0	None
Rock group G (figure 4)	36	8	One milling area with superimposed mortars(6)
Rock group H (figure 5)	42	21	Five milling areas with superimposed mortars(6).
Rock group I (figure 5)	0	8	None
Rock group J (figure 4)	60	15	Two milling areas with superimposed mortars(2)
Totals:	289	109	

"Milling areas" includes both slick and shallow depression milling elements.

(33)

TABLE 3

Dimensional Data and Artifact Distributions

Artifact	Number	Maximum Size (mm.)			Average Size (mm.)			Weight grams	Depth inches
		L.	W.	T.	L.	W.	T.		
Points									
Type 1	212	40.0	21.0	---	23.5	14.2	----	0.6-1.5	0-54
Type 2	72	40.0	20.0	---	24.0	14.5	---	ave. .78	0-48
Type 3	27	38.0	19.0	---	27.8	15.6	---	ave. 1.1	0-42
Type 4	1	----	----	---	26.0	12.0	---	.86	0-6
Type 5	10	30.0	19.0	---	23.5	----	---	ca. 1.0	0-18
Type 12	6	30.0	18.0	---	26.8	16.0	...	ca. 2.0	0-60
nondiag. fragments	133							-------	0-60
Knives									
Type 1	15	46.0	22.0	---	37.0	21.6	---	------	0-30
Type 2	13	48.0	25.0	---	40.1	23.7	---	------	0-36
Type 3	5	44.0	20.0	---	39.5	22.7	---	------	0-48
Type 4	11	46.0	25.0	---	40.0	22.0	---	------	0-42
Type 6	3	fragments only							0-36
nondiag. fragments	25							------	0-36

(34)

TABLE 3 (continued)

Artifact	Number	Maximum Size (mm.) L.	W.	T.	Average Size (mm.) L.	W.	T.	Weight grams	Depth inches
irregular flake knife	3	no dimensions available							0-36
utilized flake knife	4	no dimensions available							0-6
Drills									
all	12	(sizes here duplicate projectile point types 1-3 above)							0-42
Scrapers									
domed	5	82.0	68.0	21.0	25.0	25.0	17.0	-------	0-36
keeled	1	-------			48.0	33.0	45.0	-------	18-24
cortex-based	4	68.0	57.0	25.0	45.0	38.0	18.0	-------	0-42
flake	5	76.0	59.0	30.0	43.0	21.0	21.0	-------	0-12
nondiag. fragments	2	-------			-------			-------	0-30
Worked Flakes	59	no dimensions available						-------	0-54

TABLE 3 (continued)

Artifact	Number	Maximum Size (mm.) L.	W.	T.	Average Size (mm.) L.	W.	T.	Weight grams	Depth inches
Scraper Planes	2	109.0	70.0	39.0	91.0	73.0	53.0	------	ca.30
Chopper	1	-------			110.0	100.0	---	-------	0-6
Hammers	7	109.0	58.0	28.0	73.0	66.0	36.0	------	0-24
Hammer Grinder	2	(1 whole specimen)			65.0	60.0	50.0	------	0-18
Mortars									
portable bedrock	9 289	fragments only------- max. dia. 300.0; depth 250.0; av. dia. 160.0; av. depth 100.0							0-42 surface
Pestles	8	303.0	156.0	109.0	86.0	61.0	54.0	-------	0-42
Milling Stones									
portable deep basin	12	435.0	367.0	115.0	416.6	312.6	99.0	-------	0-30

(36)

TABLE 3 (continued)

Artifact	Number	Maximum Size (mm.) L.	W.	T.	Average Size (mm.) L.	W.	T.	Weight grams	Depth inches
portable shallow basin	6	(1 whole specimen)			293.0	205.0	75.0	------	0-24
bedrock									
slicks and		305.0	180.0	---	140.0	200.0	----	------	surface
metates	109	600.0	450.0	---	225.0	150.0	----	------	surface
Manos									
1-UU	6	115.0	104.0	72.0	84.0	72.0	46.0	------	0-42
2-UB	11	122.0	97.0	51.0	81.0	57.0	47.0	------	0-48
3-WB	5	142.0	85.0	50.0	107.0	85.0	41.0	------	0-24
4-SB	39	135.0	96.0	43.0	78.0	48.0	38.0	------	0-48
5-MP	7	124.0	79.0	69.0	100.0	89.0	65.0	------	0.30
6-SU	5	no whole specimens						------	0-24
nondiag. fragments	15	------			------			------	0-42
Edge-ground Cobble	1	------			98.0	80.0	36.0	------	----
Smoothing Stone	3	50.0	39.0	18.0	37.0	37.0	26.0	------	12.42

TABLE 3 (continued)

Artifact	Number	Maximum Size (mm.) L.	W.	T.	Average Size (mm.) L.	W.	T.	Weight grams	Depth inches
Arrowshaft Stone	1	50.0	39.0	18.0	37.0	37.0	26.0	-------	15
Paint Stone	1	-------			-------			-------	0-6
Crystal	2	-------			-------			-------	6-42
Wand Insert	1	-------			31.0	11.0	6.0	1.3	surface
Bone Artifacts									
prob. awls	33	fragments only			-------			-------	0-48
flaking tools	2	fragments only			-------			-------	0-12
scraper ?	1	fragment			-------			-------	30-36
pendant	1	fragment			-------			-------	42-48
incised bird bone	1	fragment			-------			-------	30-36
worked fragments	21	fragments only			-------			-------	0-54

TABLE 3 (continued)

Artifact	Number	Maximum Size (mm.) L. W. T.	Average Size (mm.) L. W. T.	Weight grams	Depth inches
Shell Artifacts					
Beads					
Spire lopped					
Olivella	12	ca. 10.0 to 18.0 mm. length			0-36
Olivella					
disc	4	ca. 6.0 to 8.0 mm. dia.			0-18
Pendants					
Haliotus					
fragments	3	fragments only	------	------	6-24
Ceramic Artifacts					
Sherds	2728	all fragments	------	------	0-48
Fired clay					
pipe	7	all fragments	------	------	0-18
Miniature clay					
pipe	1	57.0 long 19.0 diameter	------	------	0-6
Fired clay					
figurines	4	all fragments	------	------	0-6
Tripod pot	1	104.0 dia. 51.0 deep	------	------	surface

(39)

TABLE 3 (continued)

Artifact	Number	L.	W.	T.	Weight grams	Depth inches
Worked sherd	1	dia. 23.0 thickness 6.0				0-6
Historic Artifacts						
Knives (steel)	2	(no dimensional data)				0-6
Trade beads	2	(blue glass disc 3.0 mm dia.				surface
		blue glass tube 4.0 mm. long, 3.0 mm. dia.)				
China/glass sherds	3	(no dimensional data)				0-6

1. Some lengths are reconstructed (estimated)
2. All measurements are estimated.
3. Measurement here is minimum rather than average size.
4. One specimen from this group is from test trench (Pauma complex).
5. Specimens recovered from test trench (Pauma complex).
6. See table 5 for potsherd distribution in site. A tiny number of sherds were found below the 30-inch level. These are believed to be a result of gopher workings.

TABLE 4

Distribution of Artifacts by Material

	Xtaline quartz	Basalt	Chert	Chalcedony	Felsite	Obsidian	Other	Total
Projectile Points								
Type 1	143	13	5	2	4	8	10	185
Type 2	61	1	–	–	–	1	1	64
Type 3	23	1	1	–	–	1	–	26
Type 4	–	–	1	–	–	–	–	1
Type 5	5	2	–	–	–	1	1	9
Type 12	3	1	–	–	–	–	1	5
nondiagnostic	109	7	2	–	4	2	9	133
Knives								
Type 1	12	–	1	–	–	–	1	15
Type 2	7	2	1	–	–	–	2	12
Type 3	4	–	–	–	1	–	–	5
Type 4	9	–	–	–	1	–	1	11
Type 6	3	–	–	–	–	–	–	3
irregular flake	–	2	–	–	1	–	–	3
utilized flake	2	–	–	–	–	2	–	4
nondiagnostic conventional forms	22	2	2	–	1	1	1	29

TABLE 4 (continued)

	Xtaline quartz	Basalt	Chert	Chalcedony	Felsite	Obsidian	Other	Total
Drills	11	-	-	1	-	-	-	12
Scrapers								
domed	-	2	-	-	1	-	2	5
keeled	-	1	-	-	-	-	-	1
flake	-	2	-	-	-	-	3	5
cortex-based	-	2	-	-	-	-	-	2
nondiagnostic	-	2	-	-	-	-	-	2
Worked flakes	50	1	1	-	1	6	-	59
Scraper plane	-	1	-	-	1	-	-	2
Chopper	-	1	-	-	-	-	-	1

Total number of chipped stone artifacts: 596
Chipped stone artifacts made of crystaline quartz: 464
Percentage of chipped stone made on quartz: 78%

(42)

The use of such bedrock mortars for the processing of acorn meal has been well documented ethnographically. For the San Luis Rey II occupation there is little question of the function and significance of these elements. Likewise, there is some ethnographic support for the use of basket hoppers in this area which would account for the small shallow mortars (Sparkman 1908: 207).

On the other hand there are no convincing ethnographic accounts that describe the other milling elements. However, it is suggested that all or most of the various kinds of grinding elements found here are essentially contemporaneous and were all used in San Luis Rey II times for the processing of different kinds of food products; small seeds on the milling surfaces and acorns in the mortars. There is a possibility—based on distribution of this element in other site contexts—that the slick surfaces predate the mortars and deeper metate-like features.

Based on ethnographic data available for the Luiseño as a whole and specifically for sites in the adjacent Pauma territory, it is possible to suggest that the larger outcrops were community milling stones with each family or other social grouping utilizing its own outcrop area. Each group then had its milling area and each family woman had her mortar or group of milling elements. The milling stones located at Silver Crest (Palomar Mountain State Park) belonging to the adjacent Pauma village were identified by Max Peters as the property of a specific family. Each family had its own "place" and each mortar hole belonged to a particular "lady". If the pattern at Molpa in protohistoric times followed that of the adjacent Pauma Village, it is likely that these "holes" were passed down from mother to daughter and were used until they became too deep to be functional. None of the mortars at Molpa appear to be especially deep, and they do not approach the size of similar mortars recorded on Palomar proper and in some of the Diegueño (Cuyamaca Complex) sites to the south.

In addition to bedrock milling-stone elements described above, one additonal feature must be mentioned. Along the upper (southwestern) margin of the site a single large basin was recorded that was outstanding

because of its extreme size. This appears to be an
outsize basin metate several times larger than any
other recorded for the area so far. At the time of its
discovery it was designated the "bathtub". White
(1963: 125) proposes that this is a place to soak skins
and to process basketry material. His informants called
it a tota patch hamish. This information has not been
confirmed by other informants and does not seem to be
included in any of the older Luiseño literature.

Pictographs

Pictographs were found in two locations at Molpa.
One group of painted elements is found on the eastern
face of Rock Outcrop A (see fig. 5). The second group
was found on an outlying boulder near the extreme southwest margin of the larger site area (see map 3, location of Paha poki).

The first group (Rock A) is nearly illegible, and
it is almost impossible to describe the individual elements. It is possible to recognize the presence of the
paintings only when light is favorable and possible to
suggest only that the elements were typical geometrical
forms described for the Luiseño in general (True 1954).
Apparently all designs were painted in red. The rock
surfaces here are quite rough, and there has been considerable spalling. It is likely that the elements
remaining are but a small part of the original panel.

The second group of designs is found on a large
boulder 20 to 30 feet in diameter and 15 feet tall. In
addition to the near vertical north and east faces there
is a small shelter with a sloping ceiling near the base
at the southeast corner of the rock. This is little
more than an overhang, but it has provided some pro-
tection from the elements, and designs found on this
part of the rock are in better state of preservation
than those on the other areas. The paintings are
found on a panel approximately 9 feet square. Only the
color red is obvious, but some black elements may have
been included originally since large portions of the
original panel have exfoliated and are no longer intact.
As with the first group, they are typical of geometric

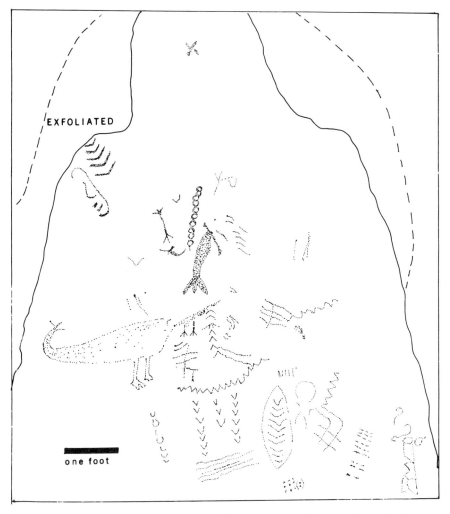

EXFOLIATED

one foot

Fig. 9. Design elements on pictograph rock location marginal to site. This is the location described by Luiseño informants as Paha-poki. (See map 2 for general location of Pahapoki relative to the site proper.)

pictographs from the Luiseño territory in general but include several human or zoomorphic elements. There does not appear to be any superimposition of elements, although it is typical to paint one design over the other in some situations. A small paint mortar has been pecked into the bedrock at the base of the over-hang. Those design elements that could be seen well enough to record are illustrated in figure 9.

Although it is obvious that this location has not been used for some time, some specific ethnographic information on the paintings was available. According to Luiseño informants this place is known generically as Paha poki (red racer's home). Essentially it was described as related to the girls' puberty rituals where rock painting is part of the normal procedure. For references describing these ritual activities see Sparkman 1908: 224-226; DuBois 1908: 93-96; and Harrington 1934: 16-22. Paintings like those at Molpa are known from several other sites of the San Luis Rey II culture (True 1954).

Petroglyphs

No petroglyphs, as we usually think of this term, were found on this site. (There are no pecked designs similar to the painted ones described above.) However, two categories of elements were noted that are consid-ered to be petroglyphs in some situations. Both are similar in form.

The first category includes those small pits or drilled holes found on the feature indicated on map 3 and figure 6 as a "rainrock". This so-called "rain-rock" is a boulder 5 feet in height pitted with hundreds of small holes (see pl. 5). This particular feature is the only one if its kind reported so far in this part of southern California. A similar one is known on Catalina Island. They are not uncommon in northern California where it is believed that the holes or pits were in some way related to ritual activities often concerned with weather control (Baumhoff 1969, personal communication). It is not known if a similar

meaning may have applied in southern California. The
Luiseño did have ritual designed to control the weather
(Raymond C. White 1956, personal communication), but
Luiseño informants present at the time the excavations
did not suggest this possibility, and one suggested that
it was a "sharpening stone" used to put points on
arrows.

The second category of elements is similar in that
they are small pecked depressions placed on bedrock outcrops and large boulders. The size of the depressions
and their placement serve to differentiate them from
the small diameter holes (usually about 1/2 inch) in
the "rainrock" feature. In this second category, the
depressions are from an inch to 2 inches in diameter
and up to 1/2 inch deep. All have been pecked and some
polished so that they look like small mortars. However, their position on vertical faces of the rocks
eliminate any kind of functional grinding use. They are
found in clusters or groups but do not seem to form
designs. At Molpa only one concentration of these depressions was located (see fig. 5). They have been reported from sites on the top of Palomar Mountain in
Pauma territory (D. L. True, field notes), and are
known to be part of the cultural pattern of the Cuyamaca
Complex in Diegueño territory (True 1970: 17).

THE ARTIFACTS

Eight hundred and eighty-six artifacts were recovered from SDi-308 (not including potsherds). These
include excavated and surface-collected items. These
implements have been classified on the basis of formal
and dimensional attributes. Function, where implied by
classification headings is assumed on the basis of
traditionally accepted criteria, and no determined
attempt was made to test these implications empirically.
In some instances the separation among classes is obviously arbitrary, and many of the described artifacts
may have been multipurpose tools.

The concept of "type" as it is used here, refers
to those clusters of attributes that seem to have cultural meaning and represent the end product of some

mental template: a socio-culturally determined form considered proper for that particular tool in that particular milieu. For some classes of artifacts the concept "type" used in this manner presents few problems. In others, we have used the term "form" rather than type. What we have categorized as a Projectile Point Type 1, for example, has a demonstrated distribution through time and space that is not random. Similar forms are found together in contexts believed to be significant. The shape and size of this tool appear to be the result of deliberate aim of the maker, recognizing that there is an acceptable range of sizes and configurations that fall within the aimed-for type. In contrast, the form of a "scraper plane" is likely to be much less significant culturally since the configuration and size of this class of tool is subject to considerable modification resulting from resharpening over a period of time.

In any case the classification suggested here is not presumed to be the final word on the subject. In order to facilitate comparisons the categories utilized correspond as much as possible to classifications used previously for this area.

Projectile Points

Six possible categories or types of projectile points have been recognized in this sample. Projectile points are defined on the basis of configuration and size. Knives and possible dart points are separated from arrow points on the basis of weight, although the dividing line is not always clear. In this assemblage, artifacts weighing more than 2 grams are considered to be either knives or dart points. Most arrow points here weigh close to 1 gram.

The outline discussion below describes each of the types believed to be represented in the assemblage. Following the heading for each type, the number of artifacts in the category is indicated in parenthesis. Dimensional data are given in table 3.

Projectile Point—Type 1 (212) (Plate 6, a-m)

Small, lightweight triangular points with concave
bases; there is some range in size and configuration although they seldom exceed 1.5 grams in weight. There
are differences in the basal configuration with V-shaped
versus U-shaped concavities. The depth of the basal
concavity varies from barely perceptible to as much as
6 mm. The sides of the point may be straight, convex
or concave. This point may be equivalent in form and
weight to the Cottonwood Triangular, Subtype b, described by Lanning (1963: 252).

Projectile Point—Type 2 (72) (Plate 6, n-t)

A small lightweight triangular point similar to
Type 1 except that it has a straight base. This is a
less common artifact than Type 1 and may represent a
variation within the Type 1 configuration. This artifact also falls within the Cottonwood series (Subtype a)
(Lanning 1963: 252).

Projectile Point—Type 3 (27) (Plate 6, u and v)

Small lightweight triangular points with convex
bases. This is not a common form and again may represent a variation within the basic Type 1 range. This
form is described by Lanning as a Cottonwood subtype
(Lanning 1963: 252).

Projectile Point—Type 4 (1) Plate 6, w)

Small triangular point with rudimentary side
notches or indentations. The base configurations of
this type tend to be concave but straight-based forms
are known. The single specimen in this assemblage has
a V-shaped concave base. This seems not to be a common
form in southern California but this may be due in part
to lack of reporting, since Type 4 points are often
lumped into a general Desert Side Notched category.

Projectile Point — Type 5 (10) (Plate 6, x-z)

Small lightweight triangular concave-based points with side notches. This is similar if not identical to Baumhoff's General and Delta subtypes of the Desert Side Notched Series (Baumhoff and Byrne, 1959: 37). As with Type 1 described above, there is variability in depth of the basal concavities and the basal configurations (V-shaped versus U-shaped).

Projectile Point — Type 12 (6) (Plate 7, a and b)

Small leaf-shaped points. This is not a common form in San Diego County and there may be little justification for separating the indicated specimens from the Type 3 category described above. Some of these specimens may be knives rather than projectiles.

Types 6, 7, 8, 9, and 10 in the series have been described for other late sites in the San Diego County upland regions but were not found at SDi-308 (True 1966). Artifacts classified as Type 11 projectile points in this earlier description have been reexamined in the present analysis. At best they are questionable projectile points, although they may have been multi-purpose tools. One artifact from this category (see pl. 6, bb) has now been reclassified as a drill, based on wear and abrasion patterns found on the tip under microscopic examination. Serrated forms of what otherwise appear to be projectile points may have been used as saws or some kind of cutting tool. Every serrated artifact from this assemblage so far examined has abrasion marks on the tips of the serrations. Similar wear or abrasion is not evident on the edges of any of the projectile points. Plate 6, z, aa, bb and plate 12, a and b, illustrate the serrated forms and wear on artifacts found at SDi-308.

In addition to the projectile point types described above, one large point or knife was recovered that is clearly intrusive. This implement is roughly triangular shaped, has a concave base and is side notched. It can be differentiated from Type 5 points on the basis of

its size. It is 45 mm. long (reconstructed), 24 mm.
wide, and 5 mm. thick. The weight is unknown but it
is clearly not in the same weight class as the Type 5
points described above. This artifact is illustrated
on plate 7, c beside a typical Type 5 point to emphasize the differences. It was found in unit J-33 in
the 24 to 30-inch level. Artifacts similar to this are
not uncommon in the Great Basin, but are exceedingly
rare in southern California upland sites. Jennings
describes this type from Danger Cave (Jennings 1957:
121), and Riddell reports on a nearly identical form
from northeastern California (Madeline Dunes side
notched) (Riddell 1960: 16). A total of 327 diagnostic
points and 133 nondiagnostic point fragments was recovered from the site; 20 points listed in the original
catalogue could not be located for the reexamination
and are not included in the present figures.

Knives

All implements believed to have been suited for
some kind of cutting function are included in this category. Three classes are recognized in the sample:
1. Bifacially flaked implements with some kind of
   conventionalized form.
2. Irregular flakes with edges modified for
   cutting or holding.
3. Utilized flakes without intentional modification.

Bifacially flaked-conventionalized forms

Forty-eight bifacially flaked tools believed to
be knives have been sorted into five conventionalized
forms that may or may not represent types. Another
thirty nondiagnostic fragments probably belong with the
above. In general, knife forms duplicate those of the
projectile points and are differentiated primarily on
the basis of size. In some instances, however, artifacts believed to be knives were marked by wear facets
and abrasion along the cutting edges.

Type 1 (15) (Plate 7, e and f)

Roughly triangular to lanceolate forms with a straight base. This is essentially an enlarged version of a Type 2 projectile point.

Type 2 (12) (Plate 7, g and h)

Roughly triangular to lanceolate form with a convex or rounded base. This is an enlarged version of a Type 3 projectile point.

Type 3 (5) (Plate 7, i and j)

Triangular to lanceolate forms with concave bases. These are similar to Type 1 projectile points except for the size.

Type 4 (11) (Plate 7, k, l, and m)

Oval- to leaf-shaped forms. Only fragments have been recovered at SDi-308, so size ranges in table 3 are mostly estimates.

Type 6 (3) (Plate 7, n and o)

A lanceolate form with a straight base. The stem end of this artifact is tapered and narrower than the center section. The sample consists only of fragments, and no dimensions other than the width are available.

Irregular flake knives (3) (Plate 8, f)

Artifacts here consist of irregularly shaped flakes of various dimensions that have been modified on one or more edges. Flaking may be bifacial but no obvious template is involved, and flaking is confined to the working edge. Irregular flaked knives probably overlap in both form and function with irregular flake scrapers.

Utilized flakes (4) (not illustrated)

In addition to irregular flakes with deliberate retouch or shaping, four flakes were catalogued that had evidence of wear or use on one or more margins. These could have functioned either as cutting or scraping tools. The small size of the sample suggests that additional specimens may have been discarded as unmodified waste flakes in the original analysis. This is considered likely since the majority of the tools in this assemblage are made of crystalline quartz and quartz flakes do not show use flaking or wear facets to the same degree as the fine-grained volcanics or cryptocrystalline materials.

Drills

Twelve artifacts (pl. 7, p-s) that were probably used for drilling purposes have been identified in the sample. No typology is suggested, but some differences are noted in configuration. Three of the specimens are fragments and look like projectile point tips with concave sides and slightly heavier than usual sections. One is an irregular flake with a drill-like projection on one end (see pl. 7, s). One small serrated specimen was previously classified as a Type 11 projectile point (pl. 6, bb). The remainder of the sample is similar to Type 1, 2, and 3 projectile points with slightly reworked tips. The similarity between the two kinds of tools suggests that a reexamination of the entire projectile point sample with a microscope might produce several more drilling, cutting, or graving implements (multi-purpose?).

Scrapers

Four basic categories of scraping tools are suggested:

Domed scrapers (5) (Plate 8, b, and h; Plate 9
b and d)

Tools classed as domed scrapers are round to oval
or elongate forms with a plano-convex cross section.
The marginal flaking tends to be steep, and most if not
all of the dorsal surfaces have been modified or shaped
by flaking. Domed scrapers are not common in the SLR
complex and some may be intrusive from an earlier component. All are made made of fine-grained rock, probably of volcanic origin. All specimens in this sample
had indications of wear on one or more edge or surface.
Usually this was evident as small abraded or polished
areas on the planar surface. Further, in some instances
abraded or worn surfaces were present on the upper
(dorsal) part of the artifact, usually along the flake
scar intersections. The patterns of wear here suggest
more than one kind of use, sometimes multiple uses for
the same artifact.

Keeled scrapers (1) (Plate 11, d)

A high-backed oval or elongate form with a sharp
keel or dorsal ridge. The single specimen is made of
basalt. There are pronounced wear facets on <u>several</u>
surfaces.

Cortex-based flake scrapers (4) (Plate 8, a and d, top
and bottom views; Plate 9, a)
Oval to irregular flakes with intact cortex on one
surface. The cortex side is polished and striated
suggesting use as a planar surface for either scraping
or smoothing. However, all edges and surfaces were
utilized and flake scars on the dorsal side also ex-
hibited wear facets and polish.

Flake scrapers (5) (Not illustrated)

Oval- to irregular-shaped flakes with modification
on one or more edge or surface. Some specimens are reworked flakes knocked off of planes or heavier tools in
the resharpening process. Irregular flake scrapers are
differentiated from utilized flakes on the basis of

what appears to be deliberate shaping or development of a working edge as opposed to use of existing nonmodified edges.

Worked flakes (59) (Not illustrated)

This includes all the chipped stone fragments that cannot be placed in any specific tool type category. They may be unrecognizable fragments of knives, scrapers, and projectile points or they may be unfinished pieces.

Scraper Planes

Scraper planes are defined as heavy-duty scraping or planing implements characterized by a well-defined planar surface. The shape of this tool may vary from round to irregular and from well-shaped artifacts to cobble fragments with minimal modification. Usually a planar surface was made by striking a large flake from a core or cobble. The margins of the remaining core were then trimmed to create a working edge at the intersection of the marginal flake scars and the planar surface. This trimming was done by percussion, and modification or shaping seems to have been minimal consistent with the creation of an adequate cutting edge. It is this edge that is important and not some predetermined culturally defined form since both the size of the tool and to some degree its shape were changed through use as they were resharpened. This is a hand-held tool, and the size ranges are those convenient for working with one hand. The overall configurations for scraper planes are about the same as those of domed scrapers, the difference being essentially one of size. Because scraper planes are reduced in size through time due to sharpening and wear, there is no clear cut line between the smaller scraper planes and the larger domed scrapers. In some samples there is more than one recognizable form within the larger class, and some kind of typology may be useful. In this sample, however, only two artifacts (pl. 11, a, b, and c) are considered to be in the scraper plane class. Both were recovered from the test trench off site and are part of the Pauma Component.

Choppers

A single artifact (not illustrated) probably representing some kind of chopping tool was recovered in
the upper level of the midden at SDi-308. This is a
fractured cobble modified or retouched on one side to
form a crude cutting edge. It is made of a basaltic
material.

Hammers

Seven artifacts (not illustrated) were found that
probably represent pounding tools of one kind or another. One (116-767) was identified by a Luiseño informant as an "anvil or nutcracker".

Hammer-Grinders

Two artifacts (pl. 11, e) were found that seem to
be multipurpose tools with well-defined battered areas
plus wear facets suggesting some kind of grinding use.
The first is a granitic material, the other a quartzite
or sandstone.

Milling-Stone Elements

Included in this large category are tools used to
grind and process food, pigments or whatever. It includes both bedrock and portable elements.

Bedrock mortars have been described previously as
features.

Mortars (9) (Not illustrated)

Nine fragments of portable mortars were recovered
from the excavations. Three of these may be from the
same artifact. For the most part the fragments are
too small to suggest a typology or to permit the description of the whole mortar. Some fragments suggest
shaping only on the interior surface, others look as

though they might have been shaped on both surfaces.
None appears to have been decorated.

Pestles (8) (Plate 9, e and f; Plate 10, a, b, and c)

Pounding tools used with the above fall into two
categories: ordinary pestles used for pounding acorn
meal and other vegetable materials in both bedrock and
portable mortars (pl. 9, e and f), and shaped ceremonial
pestles used for the preparation of ritual materials
(pl. 10, a, b, and c). The ordinary pestles are
usually unshaped cobbles, roughly triangular in outline
and often heavy enough to necessitate two-hand use.
The only modification is a flattened pounding surface
on the tip. Those considered to be ceremonial, in contrast, are finely finished, shaped on all surfaces and
are relatively small artifacts. Ceremonial pestles are
described in numerous Luiseño ethnographic contexts.
Artifacts identical to those recovered from Molpa were
so identified by Luiseño informants (Max Peters 1958,
personal communication) as ceremonial pestles used with
the tamyush (a small mortar used in several ritual activities). Sparkman (1908: 207) refers to a pestle used
with the tamyush: "the pestle of these mortars is also
neatly shaped and polished". The most often cited use
for the tamyush is to pound the Jimson weed root
(Datura) for the boys puberty rites. All specimens are
granitic rock except one which is schist.

Metates (Milling Stones) (24) (Not illustrated)

Two categories of milling stones are recognized:
(1) shallow basined or slabs, (2) deep basined. In
both categories there is a range of depth so that one
might find a continuum under some circumstances. In
most instances, however, those artifacts designated as
deep basined are clearly distinct from the shallow basined forms. All specimens are granitic except one
which is a kind of sandstone. The deep-basined forms
duplicate milling stones found in the Pauma Complex and
La Jolla Sites over much of San Diego County. Only
four of the specimens are whole or nearly so. Of these,
one has been "killed". All complete or nearly complete

specimens came from the test trench area (Pauma complex).

Manos (88) (Plate 10, d)

Hand stones used with the metates described above have been sorted into seven categories. Whether any of these groupings is in fact a "type" is not known. Most of the recognized forms probably represent stages in the development of a single type — some specialized — usage must be considered as a possibility, however.

Unshaped uniface — Unworked cobbles with wear surface on one side only.

Unshaped biface — Unworked cobbles with wear surfaces on two sides.

Wedge shaped biface — Shaped tools with wedge-shaped cross section. May have three grinding surfaces in some instances.

Shaped biface — Shaped cobble with wear on two surfaces; sometimes edges show wear as well as shaping.

Mano with pestle end — Shaped cobble with wear surfaces and pounding end combined.

Shaped uniface — A shaped cobble with wear surface on one side only.

Edge-ground Cobble

A single artifact (pl. 11, f) that falls into this category was recovered. The original analysis described this implement as a mano. Its function is unknown. In southern California edge-ground cobbles seem to be most often associated with milling-stone complexes, although they probably are also part of the San Luis Rey I inventory. The single specimen from Molpa is made on an andesitic cobble imported from the coastal region and has grinding on two edges. The surfaces have some evidence of polish and are marked by striations suggesting use as a rubbing or smoothing tool where some abrasion might be expected. This implement was recovered from the area near rock C. Informants reported that this was a "pottery anvil" or a "nutcracker". Such use is possible, but this element is typical of nonpottery culture patterns in other regions.

Smoothing Stones

Three artifacts (not illustrated) were recorded as smoothing stones or polishing stones. In most cases this kind of tool is a small "mano"-type implement or a cobble with slight wear polish on one or more surfaces. These were no doubt multipurpose and in some instances served as pottery anvils. However, two of the three found in this sample were recovered from the nonceramic San Luis Rey I component of the site.

Arrowshaft Straightener

A single steatite shaft straightener (not illustrated) was recovered from Trench A, Pit 6 at a depth of 15 inches. It was recorded as being part of feature 4, and was associated with a mano, and a mano-pestle combination. The latter probably represents a ceremonial pestle used in the Toloache ritual. The feature was located under an overhanging portion of a large boulder and appeared to be a cache situation. The specimen has been misplaced and was not available for reexamination or illustration. However, it was illustrated by Iovin in 1963 (Iovin 1963: 103).

Paint Stones

A single fragment (not illustrated) of a soft black pigment was recovered from Trench J, Pit 31. It is probably a manganese compound and is faceted by use. Such material was used as face paint and for pictograph painting. It is not uncommon on San Luis Rey sites, althoug it is seldom recovered in pieces more than a few millimeters in diameter.

Crystals

Two crystals (not illustrated) were recovered that appear to have been utilized. One is clear quartz, the other black tourmaline. The quartz crystal was found in Pit 32, Trench J, at a depth of 6 to 12 inches. The tourmaline was found in Pit 30, Trench J at the 36 to 42-inch level. Both rocks are indigenous to this region. Crystals were used in several ceremonial contexts as part of ritual equipment, and crystalline quartz was the favored raw material for chipped stone tools.

Wand Insert

One lanceolate chipped implement (pl. 8, g) was recovered that to all outward appearances represents a projectile point or small knife. Flaked from a grainy basalt-like material, this artifact was identified by a Luiseño informant (Pachito) as the insert from the top of a shaman's or religious chief's ceremonial wand. As such it was both sacred and potentially dangerous. Similar elements have been reported from other southern California locales (Burnett 1944: pl. LX). The Luiseño specimens in general, however, were probably much less elaborate than the illustrated specimens from Yaqui Wells. This particular artifact was probably an element in the Chinigchinich cult which spread over southern California at a rather late date (White 1963: 94-98).

Bone Artifacts

Bone tools are not especially common in this assemblage, although a number of activities known ethnographically for the area call for the use of bone implements. The fragmented nature of the fifty-nine recovered artifacts precludes a meaningful typology.

Thirty-three fragments were recovered that are believed to represent awls or needles (awl-like tools of one kind or another). Most are tiny fragments and non-diagnostic. One piece of scapula is probably a scraping tool of some kind, and two antler tips are interpreted as flaking tools. The function of a single piece of bird bone with an incised groove is unknown (pl. 9, g).

One incised bone fragment believed to be a pendant was
recovered. This artifact is conically drilled, but is
so fragmentary that no shape or dimensions can be suggested. Twenty-one unidentified fragments are included
in the inventory. These are worked pieces of bone that
may have been parts of awls or other implements, but
are so fragmentary no identification is possible.

Ornamentation

Other than the single drilled bone fragment mentioned above, and the possible use of black pigment for
face and body paint, all ornamentation recovered is in
the form of beads and possible pendants. Most ornaments are made of shell, although two historic blue
glass beads were found on the surface. The general
scarcity of ornamentation relative to other southern
California groups suggests little or no concern for
esthetic or ritual activities. Data from ethnographic
sources, however, suggest that the present sample does
not reflect the true situation in this regard.

The nature of the Luiseño (San Luis Rey) mortuary
customs is such that a minimum of grave goods survived
the cremations, and that which does survive, is — in the
case of shell ornaments — fragmented and calcined. The
ashes of the cremated dead plus whatever grave goods
may have survived the fire are scattered. The lack of
defined cemetaries, intact cremations, or the use of
receptacles for grave goods — as is the case in the adjacent Diegueño territory — tends to reduce the chance
of recovery of such goods by archaeologists. In spite
of this, however, and a pronounced interest in ceremonial and ritual activities, a well-developed religion,
and a subsistence capable of supporting a near sedentary existence, it does seem true that the San Luis Rey
peoples did not produce the large numbers of beads and
ornaments typical of the Diegueño to the south or the
Gabrieleño and the Chumash to the north. They had
access to the sea for raw material and obviously knew
about such practices, but seemingly were little concerned. So far no bead inlaid artifacts have been recovered archaeologically, and the total number of beads

and ornaments recovered from all known San Luis Rey
sites would probably not equal the number recovered from
a single Diegueño cremation or Chumash burial. Beads
and ornaments recovered at Molpa can be placed in the
following categories:

Spire-lopped Olivella beads (12) (Plate 7, t-aa)

    Small Olivella shells with the spire ground off to
permit stringing, this is the most common bead form
found in San Luis Rey Complex sites. Not all artifacts
in this category were used as beads, however, since
some have been described ethnographically as teeth in
the figures used in the image-burning ceremony (DuBois
1905: 625; Davis 1919: 18).

Small Olivella discs (4) (Plate 7, bb-ee).

    This is a common bead form for southern California
and has been described many times elsewhere. They
appear to have been made from the sides of Olivella,
are drilled, and usually are quite small. This kind of
bead has been recovered by the hundreds from Diegueño
cremations, but is relatively scarce on San Luis Rey
sites.

Abalone pendants or large beads (3) (Not illustrated)

    On the basis of the original field notes the species
here has been identified as Haliotis cracherodii although the artifacts are very fragmentary and hardly
diagnostic. All that can really be said is that three
fragments were recovered of some kind of Haliotis pendant or ornament.

Ceramic Artifacts

    Pottery-making was practiced by the people occupy-
ing the San Luis Rey territory in late prehistoric and
protohistoric times. Potsherds are found on many of the
late sites in this area. Preliminary examination of
the pottery sample from Molpa has already been made and

the results are in print (Meighan 1959a: 36-39; Euler 1959: 42-48). The pottery indigenous to the region has been designated Palomar Brown, a local variety of a plainware with a wide distribution in upland locales in both southern California and western Arizona (Tizon Brown) (Euler and Dobyns 1958).

A total of 2,728 potsherds (table 5) was recovered from the excavations at Molpa. Of these, 2,207 were considered to be Palomar Brown (Tizon) and 21 were classified as intrusives mostly from the Colorado River basin. Of the Colorado River sherds, only the Tumco Buff variety was identified with any reliability. For the description of Tumco Buff see Colton (1958).

The pottery sample was concentrated in the upper 18 inches of the deposit. Only a few scattered sherds were recovered from the deeper levels. On the basis of this distribution it was suggested that the upper 24 inches of the deposit clearly represented the San Luis Rey component, and that occasional sherds in the lower levels were in some way intrusive. In general, we still adhere to this interpretation. The 24 to 30-inch level contained some sherds and may represent the period of time that pottery was introduced into the area. The

TABLE 5
Ceramic Distribution

	Sherds recovered	Sherds per cubic yard
0-6	1670	159.0
6-12	658	70.8
12-18	267	41.7
18-24	54	12.9
24-30	58	15.7
30-36	32	9.2
36-42	23	6.6
42-48	12	4.4
48-54	–	–
54-60	–	–

admixture may have resulted from digging activities and disturbances of the living surface at about the 24-inch level. Occasional sherds found below the 30-inch level are attributed to gopher activity. The deposit from 30 inches to sterile is considered to be a San Luis Rey I component.

Based on the recovered sample there is little that can be said about the pottery itself, other than that which has already been published. M. J. Rogers (1936) has described the ceramics for the larger San Diego County area on the basis of ethnographic information. The archaeology generally agrees with his conclusions. The Luiseño and their immediate ancestors (San Luis Rey II) confined their ceramic-making activities to a few simple forms. Storage vessels in several sizes and a bowl form used for cooking made up the majority of the inventory. There was little attempt at decoration and this was confined to an occasional red-painted design or incised rim. The relative infrequency of this latter form of decoration is suggested by the fact that only one incised sherd is reported out of the total sample from Molpa. Basket-impressed sherds found occasionally on Diegueño sites are not present here.

There is general agreement that pottery was introduced into the San Luis Rey territory at a relatively late date. However, at the present time no data are available which firmly date the actual introduction. Everything points to the Diegueño territory as the point of origin for San Luis Rey pottery and this is supported in part by the distribution of ceramics within the San Luis Rey territory. The further one moves away from the Luiseño/Diegueño boundary the less frequent the pottery becomes. Relative to the Diegueño who made a wide variety of pottery forms, probably for some considerable length of time, the San Luis Rey samples are minimal. For example, the pottery-bearing levels of SDi-308 where the concentration was the highest, produced approximately 159 sherds per cubic yard for the 0 to 6-inch level, and 70 sherds per cubic yard for the 6 to 12-inch level. In contrast at SDi-860 (a Diegueño site in the Cuyamaca Mountains), the total depth of the midden (30 to 36 inches) averaged close to 800 sherds per cubic yard. Part of this difference can be

attributed to the Diegueño practice of placing cremations in urns. This substantially increases the number
of sherds concentrated on the site if a cemetery is
included in the figures. Further, many Luiseño (San
Luis Rey) pots were cached in storage locations away
from the village proper, so that the figures based on
sherds recovered in the midden do not tell the whole
story. However, a similar storage practice prevailed
amongst the Diegueño so their total ceramic output
would also have to be increased by some factor if comparisons were to be accurate. Based on accounts by
nonprofessional collectors and nondocumented reports
on pots found over a span of the past two decades, it
would appear that the Diegueño (Cuyamaca) territory has
produced many more finds than that of the Luiseño (San
Luis Rey). From the evidence it is possible to conclude that there was both a qualitative and quantitative difference in the ceramics produced by the people
in these two territories, even though we still lack
the specific data needed to document all of the differences. The differences between the two regions suggested by the relative frequency of storage and cooking
vessels is also supported by the number of ceramic
artifact forms other than vessels. The range of ceramic
elements found in the Diegueño territory is not repeated
in the sample from Molpa. Some of the same elements are
present in both regions, but in most cases there are
significant differences in both the quantity (number
of kinds of artifacts) and the workmanship.

Fired clay pipes (7) (Not illustrated)

Seven pipe fragments were recovered from the excavations at SDi-308. Of these, four are nondiagnostic.
One is a fragment of what has been termed a "Yuman bow
pipe" in the literature (Rogers 1936: 19-21). Another
represents the flange-like handle of a bow pipe, and
the third is a midsection of a straight tubular form
similar to that illustrated by Rogers as a Luiseño tube
pipe (Rogers 1936: 50). The four nondiagnostic fragments appear to be thin well-made bowl fragments from
bow pipes, but they are too small for certain identification.

Miniature fired clay pipe (1) (Plate 10, e)

A single fired clay miniature was recovered from the test pit area near the "rainrock" feature. It is not functional and was clearly intended to be a model or toy. It is poorly fired and not very well finished. Luiseño informants suggested that this was a toy and that it had been made by a little girl. It is logical that toys were part of the local inventory. However, this is the only miniature pipe known from the San Luis Rey territory at this time. The scarcity of this element plus its provenience near what is considered to be a ceremonial feature, suggests at least one other possible interpretation. However, it is possible that the pipe is an intrusive element from the adjacent Diegueño territory where miniatures are common. A better explanation might be that it was made locally but inspired by Diegueño models since it seems to be a noncurved example of a typical Diegueño bow pipe. No specific information is available with respect to pipes, but for other miniatures in the Diegueño territory, it has been reported that they were made especially for small children, that they were presented at some ritual occasion, and that they were preserved by the children all their lives. These elements were included in the cremation fires at the time of the individual's death. The nature of the miniature elements depended upon the child. A little girl, for example, would receive ollas because that was what what she would make and use in her later life (Florence Shipek 1968, personal communication).

Fired clay figurines (4) (Not illustrated)

No whole figurines were recovered at this site. However, four pieces were found in the excavation unit near Rock Feature C that are believed to be bulbous figurine base fragments. The outer surface of the fragments was smoothed and in one instance possibly even polished. The inner part of three contained an impression of a seed probably an acorn kernel. Similar specimens have been reported from other San Luis Rey sites (True 1957: 296). The purpose of such inclusions within the figurine is not known. However, if we are willing to assume that the figurines with bulbous termination are intended to represent pregnancies in some symbolic sense, then it is not completely out of reason to suggest that they were in fact part of some ritual activities tied to increase ceremonies. Such an explanation for figurines in general and seed-containing specimens in particular is speculative and is not based on any specific knowledge of such usage, ethnographic or archaeological.

Tripod pot (1) (Plate 11, g)

A crudely made ceramic vessel was recovered from a crack in Rock A. It is molded by hand and poorly fired. The lower surface of this artifact has three impressions marking former legs or supports of some kind. Miniatures are not common among San Luis Rey ceramics and this is the only known specimen with this particular configuration. The use of supports or legs is generally conceded to be an intrusive characteristic and probably is post contact. One Luiseño informant suggested that this kind of vessel was made by a male shaman and was used as a container for a special kind of poison. In some instances —in time of war for example— men would dip their arrow tips in this concoction to make them more lethal. In other instances such a vessel could be used by a shaman to inflict magical damage on some neighboring village. The specially constructed vessel with three legs to prevent tipping was placed in some elevated spot overlooking the village to be damaged. The vapors or fumes from the concoction it contained were supposed to lead to illness or death on the part of the village occupants (Raymond White 1956, personal communication). The reliability of this explanation cannot be verified at the present time, and it would be just as logical to suggest that some child molded this vessel in play. The village was occupied in post-contact times, and models for the leg or support elements could have been available in European or Mexican intrusives.

Worked sherds (1) (Not illustrated)

A single modified sherd was recovered. It is circular, biconically drilled in the center of the disc, and has the appearance of a spindle whorl. its use in this context is not known. It may have been an ornament. Shaped sherd fragments are not common in the San Luis Rey territory but are often found in the adjacent Diegueño sites (True 1966).

Historic Artifacts

Five artifacts representing post-contact influences were recovered during the investigations at Molpa. All were surface finds or excavated from the uppermost level (0 to 6 inches).

Knives (2) (Not illustrated)

Two fragments of iron or steel knives were recovered. One had a fragment of wooden handle still attached to its tang. This suggests the possibility that it was deposited on the site after the village was abandoned since preservation in this region is poor. The second knife included only a portion of the steel blade without a tang or handle.

Trade beads (2) (Not illustrated)

Two blue glass beads were recovered from the surface. Two different forms are represented: one is disc-like, the other more tubular. These are not uncommon bead types in southern California, occurring in association with Spanish mission-period sites dating prior to 1830.

China and glass (3) (Not illustrated)

Two china and one glass sherds were recorded. One is a handle fragment probably from a cup. The others were nondiagnostic as to form. None were recognizable as to the kind of ware. The glass was amber to brown

in color and could have come from any number of sources
either during the latter stages of the Indian occupation or after the village was abandoned.

ARTIFACT DISCUSSION

The artifact assemblage described above is an adequate sample for the purpose of delineating the tool
inventory of the ceramic-bearing component of the San
Luis Rey Complex. It is probably a fair inventory of
San Luis Rey I, as well, since many of the elements are
the same. However, the line between the two components
in this sample is not clearly defined. On the basis
of the available sample we cannot say much about activities or activity areas within the village, nor can
we talk about developments through time in detail.

The functional tool categories outlined above are
reasonably well defined on the basis of ethnographic
data, and except for multipurpose usage of individual
classes of implements, the categories are probably
valid. They were further substantiated, in part at
least, by detailed microscopic examination of the artifacts with functional criteria in mind.

For the most part the traditional uses (projectile
points, drills, knives, scrapers and related tools) were
revealed by the microscopic examination, but there was
some deviation from the expected distribution of use
classes based on formal characteristics alone. Re-
examinations of the projectile point sample using a
binocular microscope, suggests that many artifacts designated as projectile points may have served as multipurpose tools or may have been artifacts other than
projectile tips. For example, in this sample, the tips
of several artifacts previously classified as projectile points were marked by abrasion and wear and had a
worn or rounded cross section. Most of the artifacts
are made of crystalline quartz and unfortunately, this
is the most difficult material for this kind of examination because quartz does not show wear facets or
abrasion marks under light use. This means that our
observations must remain tentative, especially in any
quantitative sense. However, wear facets were clear

cut and obvious on most artifacts made of material other than crystalline quartz.

As a general rule-of-thumb the nature of project-ile point use is such that wear facets or wear abrasion would not normally be present on the tip or edges of this implement. The flake scars should be sharp and well defined except for shatter caused by impact dam-age or by step flaking left from the original manufac-ture. Therefore when wear and abrasion are found on typical point forms some other use is demonstrated.

In this sample, all of the serrated "projectile points" were examined and as a result have been re-considered in terms of their function. Wear patterns here suggest use as cutting implements rather than pro-jectiles. The edges show clear-cut wear and abrasion along the tips of the serration (pl. 12, a and b). The presence of such wear seems to be consistent. For the long parallel-sided serrated artifacts occasionally found in this region, use as a light duty saw would not be unexpected, and the discovery of wear facets on the serration tips was not a great surprise. However, similar wear patterns were found on tiny triangular forms as well. The latter are clearly within the typi-cal projectile point configurational pattern and size range. Such tools must have been hafted. The fact that many points were used as knives, saws or drills does not eliminate the use of these same artifacts as projectile points in addition to other uses.

Tools classified as knives were examined in a similar manner. For the crystalline quartz specimens it was difficult to demonstrate wear facets and no clear-cut conclusions were possible. As with the pro-jectile points, however, tools made of basalt or fel-sitic materials all had some kind of wear or abrasion along one or more edges supporting classification of these tools as knives. In some cases wear was present on flake scars over the flat surfaces as well as the edges suggesting cutting through materials where abra-sion and pressure would be present on the sides as well as the cutting edge. These are of course not unique nor unusual findings. They do add weight to the cate-gorization previously set up in terms of tool types and in most instances demonstrate that artifacts called

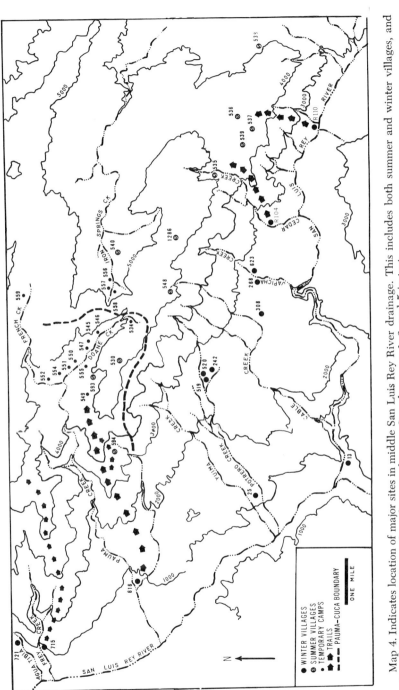

Map 4. Indicates location of major sites in middle San Luis Rey River drainage. This includes both summer and winter villages, and the trails connecting them when these are known. See also maps 1, 3, and 5 in text.

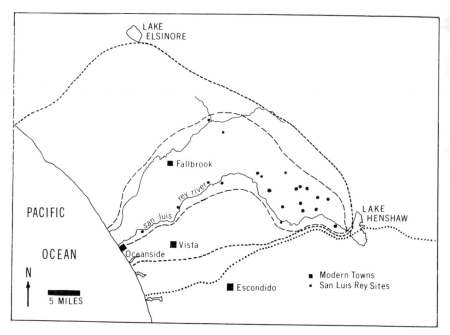

Map 5. Boundaries marking the San Luis Rey territory. The short dashed line marks the approximate boundary of the ethnographically defined Luiseño territory except that the southern boundary has been modified on the basis of new data. All of the territory here, at least, is included in the San Luis Rey I phase. The longer dashed line indicates the known distribution of San Luis Rey II sites. All of the space *above* the dotted line may be San Luis Rey I if we include the historic Cupeño and Cahuilla territory as well as the Luiseño. This is a good possibility, but has not yet been verified archaeologically.

Map 6. Categories of sites used to document the San Luis Rey pattern.

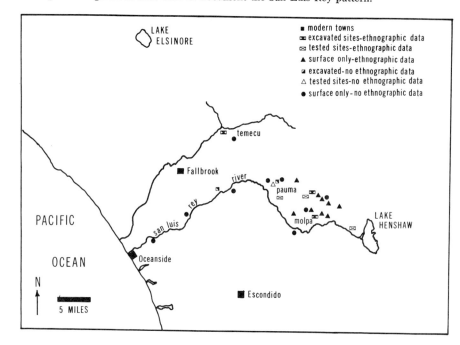

knives were indeed cutting tools and not roughed-out blanks for future reworking into some other kind of artifact. This does not mean that knives could not be multipurpose. Artifacts intended as blanks could be used in the interim as cutting tools and eventually reworked into projectile points or whatever. Implements utilized primarily as knives or intended as blanks could as well serve as casual scrapers.

Most scrapers in the sample also have wear facets and well-defined striations indicating considerable use. Such facets are found on various surfaces indicating that more than one working edge was utilized. Each tool may have served for more than one kind of operation. No attempt was made to discover or treat all of the possibilities inherent in this kind of analysis. The knife and scraper categories, for example, are too small to have any statistical value or to be significant in terms of differences in location within the site.

No so-called activity areas or special use areas within the site could be defined on the basis of this artifact sample. Our purpose was not to do a detailed lithic analysis, but rather to add a limited amount of information in support of the usual artifact categorization employed in the classification. We hoped to demonstrate use on at least some of the artifacts and this has been done.

CULTURAL GEOGRAPHY OF THE SAN LUIS REY CULTURAL PATTERN

It is not possible to define the geographic extent of the San Luis Rey cultural pattern in detail since not all the sites that might belong to this grouping have been recorded or studied. On the basis of those data that are available we suggest that the boundaries of San Luis Rey I correspond in a general sense with the ethnographically defined boundaries of the historic Luiseño, and that San Luis Rey II had a somewhat more restricted distribution within these bounds. At this point this distribution seems well enough documented and is quite firm. Whether the archaeologically defined San Luis Rey Complex extended into the historically defined Cahuilla territory is not known, although

this is considered possible if not probable. It did
not, however, extend into the historically defined
Diegueño territory to the south, which is characterized
by a separable and distinct cultural inventory. The
most obvious manifestations of San Luis Rey II are found
on those sites closest to the ethnographically defined
Luiseño-Diegueño boundary. As one moves north and west,
pottery becomes less and less common and some elements
critical to the definition of San Luis Rey II seem to
be missing. Ceramics have been reported from sites in
the Fallbrook-Temecula region (McCown 1948), but become less and less frequent as one moves northwestward
toward the Elsinore Valley and the Santa Ana Mountain
regions. Pottery is literally unknown in Gabrieliño
territory except in post-contact contexts. Map 4 shows
the summer and winter villages in the middle San Luis
Rey River drainage, and map 5 indicates the general
location of known San Luis Rey sites for the area at
large as well as suggested boundaries for the complex.
    The data supporting this geographic distribution
include:
1. Excavated samples from ethnographically known
    locations where a reasonably large amount of
    midden was examined.
2. Excavated samples from ethnographically known
    locations where the samples are limited to
    test pit excavating.
3. Excavated samples from test pit situations
    on sites with San Luis Rey characteristics, but
    lacking ethnographic confirmation.
4. Surface-collected samples from ethnographically
    known locations.
5. Surface-collected samples from sites with San
    Luis Rey characteristics but lacking ethno-
    graphic identification.
The distribution of these various site categories
is shown on map 6. These distributional data are supplemented by information in appendices A and B.
    With regard to the geographic extent of the San
Luis Rey complex, it should be noted that the sites at
Vallecitos, San Vicente, and Ramona listed as examples
of San Luis Rey II in the original report (Meighan 1954:
223), are not part of the San Luis Rey pattern as it is

Map 7. Boundaries of four Luiseño village territories on Palomar Mountain. Locates principal village (winter villages) for each community. For all of the territories except Pala this location is known from both ethnographic and archaeological data. Solid lines represent boundaries that are still recognized. Light dashed lines indicate the part of the territory where the lines tend to be uncertain. The heavy dashed line represents the boundary of the Luiseño territory. The heavy dotted line is the approximate ethnographically designated boundary of the Luiseño territory in the south. Recent data suggest that this may be in error, and that the line should be moved to the north, perhaps almost to the San Luis Rey valley in some places.

now defined. These should be included as part of the Cuyamaca complex defined for the Diegueño territory (True 1966; 1970).

House Types and Structures

No archaeologically derived information is available for any kind of architectural features in San Luis Rey territory other than those known to date from post-mission times.

Reports from farmers clearing lands within this territory in the 1930s tell of knocking down "brush huts" still surviving at that time. Ethnographic accounts suggest that the Luiseño constructed conical huts that sometimes were placed in pits up to 2 feet in depth (Sparkman 1908: 212). Shelters with similar forms are described for the mountain villages, except that here they were made of bark rather than poles and brush. At least two of these "cedar bark" shelters were still standing as late as the mid-1950s (see appendix A).

In addition to shelters used for sleeping, the Luiseño constructed ritual structures (Wamkish) which were little more than fence-like enclosures. No wamkish features have been recovered archaeologically. The same applies to sweat houses which may have been a more recent introduction.

Tools and Material Culture

Othern than those exceptions already indicated in the descriptive section (a few intrusive elements and the material recovered from the test trench), the artifacts described above are considered to be typical of the San Luis Rey II phase. For the most part the artifacts and features agree with the inventory published in the original description. The one exception to this appears to be with respect to mortuary patterns. Originally it was assumed that the cremation and urn-burial pattern recognized in the southern part of the county would extend into the north as well. Cremation urns accordingly were listed as a criterion for San Luis Rey II.

In the intervening years it has now become apparent that this is not correct, and the San Luis Rey complex people (Luiseño) did not practice urn burial. The San Luis Rey II people did cremate, but the evidence, archaeological and otherwise, suggest that the burned remains were not gathered for reburial. There is no cemetery in the formal sense of the word. The remains were left in place where they were burned or were collected as part of a ritual but not formally reburied. In the latter instance at least some of the surviving bones were ground in a mortar and mixed with water. Some of this mixture was ritually consumed by a religious practitioner and the remainder was poured into a hole in the ground (Du Bois 1908: 137).

Cultural Reconstruction

The relatively late date for the beginning of San

Luis Rey II and the obvious ties with the Luiseño permit considerable comment over and above that which can be derived from the artifacts alone. The reconstruction of the Luiseño (San Luis Rey II) cultural pattern as it must have been at the time of contact can be accomplished to a great degree from ethnographic sources supplemented by archaeological data in some instances. With few exceptions, such ethnographic reconstructions would also apply to the prehistoric segments of the San Luis Rey II phase. It seems unnecessary then, to reiterate or paraphrase a rather substantial literature dealing with Luiseño ethnography. Several key monographs and papers are available which provide the essence of the Luiseño life way, recognizing that some changes had taken place prior to the earlier contact by anthropologists, and that some aspects of this ethnography are concerned essentially with a post contact adaptation rather than an actual reconstruction of the prehistoric situation (see White 1963; Du Bois 1908; Sparkman 1908; Strong 1929; and Harrington 1934). Much of what is described in these accounts can be applied to the village of Molpa. However, the archaeology here, plus informant data not yet published, warrant some comment specific to the situation at Molpa.

The village of Molpa has been described ethnographically as "part of the village of Cuca". As near as can be determined, it was abandoned prior to the Cuca village which was occupied well into the last half of the nineteenth century. The small amount of historic refuse in the midden at Molpa and a general vagueness about the site on the part of the informants, suggests that this location was abandoned fairly early in the nineteenth century. In fact, the relationships with Cuca are not clearly defined. Molpa could have been one site out of several making up the larger Cuca settlement, or it could have been the main Cuca village, abandoned for some reason, and replaced by the sites at the present location. Another possibility is that at one point in time Molpa was an independent socio-cultural unit with the full autonomy and status of the communities of Pauma, Cuca, La Jolla, etc. (see map 7). A marked reduction of population (probably related to the mission activities at San Luis Rey) could well have made it difficult to maintain the necessary internal ceremonial relationships, and it could have set the stage for a coalition with a neighboring group. A similar situation probably prevailed for the village of Japicha, which no doubt had independent status at one time, but now is considered to be part of La Jolla. Regardless of the possibilities for earlier times, it seems clear that as of mid-nineteenth century and probably back as far as Mission times, the Molpa territory was part of the Cuca village in a social sense, if not economically. The territory of Cuca as it is now defined includes whatever territory was controlled previously by Molpa. It is likewise clear that the basic pattern of subsistence was the same for all of the Luiseño upland villages.

A key element within the subsistence pattern was the established seasonal round within a well-defined and defended territory. Map 2 shows the approximate Luiseño territorial division in the vicinity of Molpa. The concept of a seasonal round in the traditional use of the term has to be modified somewhat since the pattern here actually includes two or more permanent base camps and a number of possible temporary satellite gathering or hunting stations attached to each of the base camps. Only one base camp and its attached stations would be occupied at any given time. One base camp the main village was a winter location (in this case, the village of Molpa). The other base camp was occupied in the summer and fall during the hunting and acorn harvesting seasons. There is evidence suggesting that the occupants of a main village (winter) moved into the mountains in the spring, splitting up into lineage or sib-based groups, with each such group occupying a separate location and exploiting its own sources of vegetable resources. These separate encampments were of course within the larger territory claimed by the village as a whole. This kind of pattern seems to be indicated for the Pauma community and probably was utilized by the Cuca/Molpa peoples as well. In this latter case, however, it is not certain which of the mountain sites should be included, since the Cuca/Molpa-La Jolla boundaries are not well defined in some areas. However, at least two and possibly three important mountain villages seem to be within the Cuca territory. One of these

(Pavala) has been definitely identified as a Cuca village (Sparkman 1908: 192). Another site is located
well within the Cuca mountain territory and must have
been part of the Cuca village complex (Chatpopusa).
The third village is <u>probably</u> in the Cuca territory,
but was not identified directly as such during the investigations, and no Luiseño name was recorded for this
site. (The major villages here are located on maps 2
and 4.)

Although the subdivision of the main village into
kin-based groups in the summer camps cannot be documented specifically for Molpa, there is no question of the
basic winter and summer relocations. The entire village population spent little more than half of the year
in the winter village. From four to six months, depending upon the nature of the weather and "crops", was
spent in the mountain camps. In spite of this movement
by entire villages, we stress the lack of mobility and
the sedentary characteristics of this pattern. Each
major San Luis Rey village included a substantial number of individuals, and these individuals were supported by a relatively small territory. Unfortunately,
actual population figures are not available for the prehistoric period and figures published for later times
may be in error for various reasons. White (1963: 110)
suggests that each of the major Luiseño (San Luis Rey
II) villages included some 200 individuals. This figure is believed to be on the high side and it seems unlikely that Molpa, for example, supported more than 100
persons at any one time. Even at the lower figures,
however, this is a substantial number of people for the
size of the territory. No part of any village territory
was more than a half day's travel from either of the
base camps, so that most if not all collecting could be
done without the necessity of temporary field camps.
This concentrated the activities within each territory
at the main villages. The possibility that these villages were relocated on occasion is suggested (possible
move from Molpa to Cuca), but we do not know whether
this was a village relocation or a consolidation of two
existing villages.

In any case, it seems clear that the mountain camps
should be seen as part-time, seasonally occupied

sedentary villages, not as temporary hunting camps, and
not as part of a mobile population ranging over the
mountain in some kind of random-gathering type of subsistence.

During the summer months then, Molpa would have been
unoccupied, and coversely no one would stay over in the
mountain camps during the winter. Most essential activities were carried on in both localities, and so far
as can be determined the cultural materials (tools) recovered from the two ecological zones are seemingly the
same. However, most of the important ceremonial activities were probably carried on in the winter villages
(main village). No pictographs, for example, have been
recorded for any of the mountain villages, but they are
an important adjunct to all of the lowland winter villages.

Major Sites in Lowland Contexts
(Winter Villages San Luis Rey II)

Site SDi-721

Location: The Agua Tibia Creek drainage in the ex-
              treme northwest corner of section 32,
              Township 9 south, Range 1 west, Pala
              quadrangle 7 1/2' series (see map 4).

Affiliation: San Luis Rey II. No Luiseño designation
              is available for this site and its posi-
              tion in the overall settlement pattern is
              not clear.

Comment: Small but well-developed midden area with
              clear-cut San Luis Rey II characteristics.
              A test pit was excavated to sterile soil
              and the midden is certainly greater than
              30 inches deep over most of the area,
              which is about 70 feet wide and some 100
              feet long. Several large boulders on the
              site contain bedrock mortars. Placement
              of this village poses some problems. It
              is seemingly not claimed by the Pauma

group, although they allude to this region as being theirs. Likewise ties with the Pala group seem to be weak or lacking altogether (based on current ethnographic information). The warm springs located a short distance away (Agua Tibia) are frequently mentioned, however, and the area at large is important in the Luiseño mythology and history. Informants suggest that there was a major village at Agua Tibia in earlier times. Because of entry restrictions by the owners of this property it was not possible to confirm or deny the presence of this village. Some indication of prehistoric activity has been located in the area, but whether or not it represents the remains of a major winter village is not clear. As a hypothesis we propose that in prehistoric times the specific Agua Tibia locale was primarily a ceremonial location, rather than a regular winter village. Following the mission secularization the hot springs area was occupied as part of a new dispersed settlement pattern and a different life style. The adjacent site (SDi-721) appears to have been a prehistoric winter village of a community (now extinct) occupying the territory between the communities of Pala and Pauma. The community of Japicha adjacent to the community of La Jolla was similar. Japicha is still remembered as a community even though it ceased to function as a group some time ago. The relationships between Cuca and Molpa also are probably part of a similar pattern whereby there is some consolidation of territory in relatively recent times with the abandonment of previously important living areas. A situation such as this at SDi-721 could account for the apparent confusion over jurisdiction of the adjacent mountain territory (see

appendix A, site Palomar 14). Further
there is an indication from Pauma informants that: (1) the general area between
Pauma Creek and the Agua Tibia area was
part of the Pauma domain; (2) people from
that area had come to the main village at
Pauma at an earlier time and more or less
asked to be taken in (White 1963: 97).

Site SDi-715

Location: The Frey Creek drainage in the northwest
              1/4 of section 32, Township 9 south, Range
              1 west.

Affiliation: San Luis Rey II. The locality here is
              designated as Sulpa by Sparkman (1908:
              192).   Sparkman's reference is to the
              location "where J. Frey lives". The old
              Frey house (no longer standing) marked
              the location of the prehistoric village.
              Although it is still speculative at this
              point, this area may have been the pre-
              historic territory of the Soktchum line
              now considered to be part of the Pauma
              group (Ray White and R. Pachito 1955, per-
              sonal communication).

Comments: See comment from site SDi-721 above. Re-
              lationships between SDi-715 and the Pauma
              village are not clear, but the area itself
              is claimed by surviving Pauma people. The
              archaeological site represented here was
              literally destroyed early in the present
              century by leveling for house construction
              and attempts to farm in the area. As re-
              cently as 1949 several mortars and numer-
              ous manos could be seen lined up around
              the margins of the old houseyard area.
              Chipping waste, occasional artifacts, and
              midden deposit were clearly visible at
              that time. Pottery was present in the

midden and was recovered from several satellite locations adjacent to the village proper. No formal collections or testing was done at this time because of restrictions by the owner. Additional construction and clearing in the mid-1950s obliterated most of the remaining evidence. In spite of a dearth of specifically described artifacts, there is no question but this site belonged with the San Luis Rey II pattern.

Site SDi-616

Location: Southeast side of Pauma Creek near its junction with Jaybird Creek (see map 4).

Affiliation: San Luis Rey II. This is the prehistoric/ protohistoric winter village of the Pauma community.

Comment: A substantial portion of the midden here was washed away during the 1916 flood. Much of what remains has been damaged by orchard planting and cultivation over the past several decades. Test pits and cut banks indicate a midden depth of 36 to 42 inches. Surface collections were made systematically from this locality over a period of fifteen years. (More detailed descriptions of the artifacts will be provided in a future work.) At the present time no features have survived. Several large boulders containing mortars were "washed away" during the flood and numerous "portable" mortars were collected from the bed of Pauma creek in the years following. No house pits have survived, but ranchers in the area report knocking down "structures" when the land was cleared the first time for planting (Ken Maynard 1950, personal communication).

Site SDi-25

Location: Potrero Creek drainage about 1/2 mile
              east of the road junction at Rincon (see
              map 4).

Affiliation: San Luis Rey II. This village area be-
              longs to the people of Cuca. Its status,
              however, is not clear. To date no ex-
              cavations have been made and surface col-
              lections have been minimal. The site is
              known as Ahuya (see Sparkman 1908: 192;
              Kroeber 1925: pl. 57).

Comment: The site affiliation with the people from
              Cuca is documented ethnographically
              (Henry Rodriguez 1954, personal communi-
              cation). Examination of the midden and
              surface artifacts support a San Luis Rey
              II designation, but the place of this site
              in the larger pattern is not clear. In-
              formants have referred to this as a
              "refugee" area. This is the place the
              Cuca people came to live when they were
              removed from their village by the new
              owners of the land in the early to mid-
              nineteenth century. This notion is con-
              sistent with available data, but there
              are indications that the site was in use
              a great deal longer than this. It is sug-
              gested, based on minimal archaeological
              investigation, that (1) this was also a
              San Luis Rey I site; (2) use of the area
              in early San Luis Rey II times was minimal
              and that the people living here were con-
              solidated into the Cuca community during
              the climax of the San Luis Rey II period;
              (3) it was abandoned during this climax
              period except for very occasional use,
              and; (4) it was reoccupied during historic
              times following the removal of many of the
              Cuca people from the Potrero. Extensive

work would be required to test this pro-
posal, but it is consistent with what is
known and should be considered a reasonable
possibility.

Site SDi-13

Location: San Luis Rey River drainage in southwest
1/4 of section 36, Township 10 south,
Range 1 west (see map 4).

Affiliation: San Luis Rey II. The situation here probably parallels that of SDi-25 described
above with an early San Luis Rey I occupancy followed by a period during which
minimal use was made of the site. The
site or its immediate vicinity was probably reoccupied in late protohistoric
times. While it is not possible to fit
this location into the pattern with precision, it seems that it must have been
one of several small villages in the
Rincon/Potrero Creek area that were grad-
ually consolidated into the Cuca village
complex during the climax period of San
Luis Rey II. No ethnographic name was
obtained for this locality.

Comment: The midden here is obscured by a thin
cover of outwash from the adjacent slope.
Under the outwash there is a considerably
altered soil marked by chipping waste,
artifacts, and substantial evidence of
fire. In places where the midden is exposed (road grading) artifacts can often
be recovered following a rain. No system-
atic archaeology has been done here other
than surface collecting on a limited scale.
An adobe ruin on the slope just above the
midden probably represents early historic
Luiseño occupancy of the site. Occasional historic artifacts have been recovered

along the upper margins of the midden area

Site SDi-242

Location: A large boulder outcropping in the Potrero
             Creek drainage in the northwest 1/4 of
             section 20, Township 10 south, Range 1
             east (see map 4).

Affiliation: San Luis Rey II. This place is called
             Cuca and is the key village in the Cuca
             community.

Comment: Because people are still living close to
             this location investigation over the years
             has been kept to a minimum to avoid both-
             ering them. Enough work has been done,
             however, to clearly identify this as a San
             Luis Rey II site. There is a dark well-
             developed midden, with chipping waste and
             numerous bedrock grinding features typical
             of the area at large. Artifacts are rare
             because the local inhabitants have picked
             the surface for fifty years or more. Oc-
             casional potsherds can still be found, and
             artifacts from this locality are clearly
             San Luis Rey II in character. Further, the
             ethnographic identification of the spot as
             a key site in the Cuca complex has been
             confirmed by several different informants
             over a period of some twenty years. This
             is where the people from the Potrero lived
             before they were forced to leave the new
             owners of the Cuca Rancho (Henry Rodriguez
             1954, personal communication). The site
             was abandoned somewhere near 1870, and
             except for one family, all Indians here
             moved down the hill to the Rincon area.

Site SDi-519

Location: Potrero Creek drainage at the point where it

crosses the La Jolla Indian reservation line. The elevation is 2,560 feet (see map 4).

Affiliation: Probably San Luis Rey II. Investigations so far indicate that this is one of several components belonging to the Cuca village. This is not certain, however, and occupancy during San Luis Rey II times could have been minimal. No ethnographic data have been recorded for this specific site. Survivors tend to include this as part of the Cuca village with no qualifications.

Comment: The site area here appears to be quite extensive. Its exact boundaries, however, are unknown because of heavy vegetation and considerable modification of parts of the area at an earlier time (road and house construction). Bedrock mortars are present but not in great concentrations. The midden here is dark, ashy and well developed. Chipping waste and artifacts can be recovered from areas where the soil has been exposed. Restrictions by the owner and heavy vegetation have kept collecting activities to a minimum. The artifacts so far available place this site clearly in the San Luis Rey pattern. It may well have been more typically San Luis Rey I than II, however, and only excavation will clarify this relationship.

Site SDi-520

Location: Potrero Creek drainage western boundary of the Cuca Grant. The elevation here is about 2, 750 feet (see map 4).

Affiliation: San Luis Rey II. This is another site almost certainly belonging to the Cuca

village. So far, no name other than Cuca
has been reported for this locality.

Comment: This site is clearly separated geographically from SDi-242 (Cuca proper), but both
are in the same general area. Site
SDi-520 may be an extension of SDi-519.
The two middens are clearly separated, but
there is a scatter of artifacts along
Potrero Creek for close to 1/4 mile from
both sites. Evidence available so far
suggests that the occupancy of SDi-520 was
more recent than SDi-519. The midden at
SDi-520 is dark ashy, and well developed
and includes ample amounts of chipping
waste and numerous artifacts. When the
grass cover is absent artifacts are common on the surface. However, most of the
time the area is not exposed and surface
collecting is limited to rodent mounds
and occasional bare patches of ground.
Its depth has not been tested. It is not
certain whether this locality was abandoned at the same time as Cuca. It has been
reoccupied during historic times, however,
and has the remains of a house over a portion of the midden deposit. Use of this
site was probably tied to the water supply.
When Potrero Creek was dry, activities
tended to be shifted to SDi-242, the spring
there being much more reliable than the
flow in Potrero Creek.

Site SDi-268

Location: A small knoll in the northwestern part of
the Cuca Rancho Grant. The southeastern
1/4 of section 2, Township 10 south,
Range 1 east. The elevation is 2,700 feet
(see map 4).

Affiliation: San Luis Rey II. This was an important

locality in the settlement of Japicha.

Comment: A small site with moderate midden development compared with the village at Molpa. Still there is ample evidence of protohistoric-prehistoric occupancy. Three recognizable locations are included. The first has the most obvious evidence of a midden development. Here small moundlike features and depressions appear to be remains of previous structures. At least one of these features is almost certainly the remains of an adobe house structure of historic age. An informant (Mabel Subish 1956, personal communication) confirms that this place was occupied by an old woman whose house is gone. Almost all of this part of the site was destroyed during the 1950s as a result of a road realignment. Area 2 on this site was up the slope away from the highway and was not disturbed. Here the primary feature is a bedrock exposure with several mortars. Some soil alteration is evident here as well. Chipping waste and occasional artifacts can be found on the surface. A possible house pit depression is located on the southerly side of the described bedrock feature. Area 3 (some 25 yards to the southeast) includes another bedrock exposure and several smaller mortars. No excavations were made on this site. Some surface collections were made during the highway construction. The artifacts are typically San Luis Rey II in character.

Site SDi-623

Location: Japicha Creek drainage near the Cuca Rancho boundary. The elevation is 2680 feet (see map 4).

Affiliation: San Luis Rey II. Although investigation
                here has been minimal because the area is
                still occupied by Luiseño people, this is
                clearly part of the Japicha settlement.

Comment: Bedrock mortars are present along with
                some midden. No collections were made.
                (Eberhart n.d.: 6) reports a single
                scraper taken from this site and suggests
                that it is a San Luis Rey I site. No
                ethnographic information was obtained per-
                taining to this specific location. One
                informant gave the name wow-kila to the
                adjacent area to the east and south
                (Romulo Sobenish 1958, personal communi-
                cation). Although it has not been con-
                firmed, hints from teenage Luiseños
                suggest that this area includes pre-
                historic remains and may well be the main
                occupation area of the Japicha settlement.
                Future work with San Luis Rey settlement
                patterns will call for additional surveys
                and clarification of this point.

Site Rincon 104

Location: East side of Cedar Creek (La Jolla Creek)
                at an elevation of 2600 feet (see map 4).

Affiliation: San Luis Rey II. This is the principal
                winter camp of the La Jolla people.

Comment: Local informants refer to this place as
                "old La Jolla", "The place where we used
                to live in the old days" (Albert Sterling,
                Wilbert Nelson 1955, personal communi-
                cation). Evidence at the location con-
                firms this as an important prehistoric
                village site. The midden is dark and ashy
                and contains numerous artifacts and
                scattered chipping waste. Bedrock mortars
                were present. Because of its location

within the reservation, few non-Indians have visited this location and artifact collectors are unwelcome. Thus collections from this site are extremely limited. Nevertheless, enough data were gathered and enough observed to state clearly its position in the overall San Luis Rey pattern.

Site Rincon 110

Location: San Luis Rey River drainage below Henshaw Dam. The elevation is 2400 feet (see map 4).

Affiliation: San Luis Rey II. This location is known as Yuil-ka.

Comment: Informants at the present time do not refer to this as a principal village, but obviously it was a village of some importance in either prehistoric or protohistoric San Luis Rey times. Based on its location this site should be seen as part of the protohistoric La Jolla settlement in the larger sense, recognizing that in earlier times it was probably an autonomous community. The recovery of historic artifacts indicates some occupancy in post-mission time. Whether this is a location occupied only in protohistoric and historic times as a result of a post-contact dispersal, or whether it was reoccupied in historic times as part of a changing subsistence base following the collapse of the missions is uncertain. Informant reference to "garden spots belonging to our village" in other contexts is noted here. This could have been a "garden area" belonging to La Jolla, or simply a place occupied prior to an amalgamation during the climax of San Luis Rey II times, and later reoccupied after historic times when the basic village patterns were beginning to break down.

The site here has at least two separable areas of concentration. The lower midden, adjacent to the San Luis Rey river proper, appears to be the richer in terms of artifact concentration. It is clearly San Luis Rey II, although road construction has destroyed a significant portion of the site. The second midden area is located higher on the slope on a bench next to a small canyon draining part of the Pine Hills area of Mount Palomar. Test pits in this upper part indicate a depth of 30 inches of dark ashy midden. Artifacts, however, are not common, and potsherds tend to be scarce. A trail complex connects this locality with the Dyche Valley-Pine Hills area on Palomar. This relationship is shown on map 4.

3. DATING AND COMPARISONS

Investigations at SDi-308 (Molpa) permit some additional comments on the most recent prehistoric cultural phase in northern San Diego County, California. The deepest levels of this site appear to be consistent with the San Luis Rey I sample described from the type site SD-132 (Meighan 1954). The artifacts recovered from the test trench excavated along the northwest margins of the site are typical of the early milling-stone complex found in this region (True 1958: 255-263). This milling-stone component is clearly distinct from the San Luis Rey material. The present report is directed toward the San Luis Rey II component, and the more precise definition of this phase was the prime objective of the investigation. Suggested time relationship between the various complexes known for this area so far are presented in figures 1 through 4.

DATING

The nature of the recovered artifact assemblages and the ethnographic information available—both for the area at large and for the site in particular—indicate that San Luis Rey II is the terminal phase of the late prehistoric/protohistoric occupation in this area, and that SDi-308 was occupied well into historic times. Present estimates based on glass bead types and informant data suggest that it was abandoned sometime in the first two decades of the nineteenth century. Other SLR II villages in the area were occupied for several decades after Molpa was abandoned. In general, it seems that this phase of Luiseño culture history had terminated not later than the 1870s for the territory in general. The terminal end of San Luis Rey II, then, is defined historically and presents few problems. The beginning, however, is not clearly indicated by the data presently available, and its duration is not known.

By definition, the beginning of San Luis Rey II is marked by the introduction of ceramics into the area. This
is an arbitrary boundary and culturally may have had
little significance since San Luis Rey I inventory is
nearly identical to that of San Luis Rey II, at least
during the latter part of the SLR I occupation. In any
case the key to the temporal definition of the San Luis
Rey II phase is tied to the introduction of pottery into
the area, although there are other elements that serve
to differentiate the phases or subphases. Meighan
(1954: 223) has suggested that San Luis Rey II began
about 1750 and continued to 1850. The assumption at
that time (1954) was that pottery had not been introduced into the Luiseño territory until after contact.
At the present time there are still reasons to think
that this introduction was quite late in time, but we
have no real basis for suggesting just how late. It is
logical to assume that the introduction was by diffusion
from Diegueño territory to the south, but the possibility that some influences originated in the adjacent
Cahuilla territories should also be recognized. In
either case,however, we have no empirical evidence to
support any specific dating for this event. Not only
are we unable to document the entry of pottery into
northern San Diego County, but present data do not provide the basis for anything more than a guess for the
introduction of ceramics into the area at large. Estimates presently in print for the upland San Diego County
region are for the most part based on cross dating from
the lower Colorado River area. Since little is known
of this latter area archaeologically, and almost nothing
has been published which established firm dates for the
cultural sequence there, extrapolations from the Colorado
River ceramic sequence to the upland regions of San
Diego County can hardly be considered definitive for
dating purposes.

A cursory survey of the literature at this writing,
and a rather detailed search some four years ago indicates that investigations have been carried on at
less than half a dozen sites for the entire lower
Colorado region. Only two of these (Willow Beach and
the Bouse site) appear to have been stratified with sig-
nificantly different occupational or cultural levels

(Schroeder 1961; Harner 1958). Several C-14 dates have
been published for the Willow Beach sequence. These
provide the only direct dating for this entire region.
Recognizing the possible uncertainties of a small series
of C-14 dates from only one site, it is clear that the
temporal aspects of the lower Colorado cultural sequence are still largely undetermined. Cross dates
have been suggested based on excavations at the Bouse
site, tying intrusive sherds there to the Hohokam sequence —which at the time, was itself dated by cross-
referencing to the Anasazi sequence. It is our
contention then that until the introduction of ceramics
into the lower Colorado has been documented in considerably more detail and with a great deal more precision,
any attempt to use the Colorado River sequence to verify
the beginnings of ceramics in the San Diego County sites
will be futile. Those dates presently in print from
marginal areas, which do fall into the later prehistoric time periods, provide little insight into the solu-
tion of the larger problem.

Lacking a firm chronology for the introduction of
ceramics to the Diegueño or their ancestors, and lacking dated stratigraphic sequences in the San Luis Rey
territories, we are hard pressed to suggest a beginning
date for San Luis Rey II. It now seems likely that San
Luis Rey II had a duration in excess of the original
estimate, but we have no satisfactory way of telling
just how much more. We base this conclusion on several
lines of reasoning. For example, it would appear that
San Luis Rey components tend to average some 24 to 30
inches in depth. Taking the smaller figure and recognizing that these villages were occupied only slightly
more than half of the year, and that for each lowland
midden there is a comparable one located at the summer
camps on the mountain, we can suggest that the actual
depth of an average San Luis Rey II midden component
will be at least 48 inches —again to be conservative,
say with a minimum of 36 inches of pottery-bearing deposit. We are well aware that midden accumulation rates
cannot be used to establish absolute dates but it does
take appreciable time to accumulate 36 inches of midden
under circumstances of limited outwash and alluviation,
and in situations where the durable organic refuse

(shellfish, etc.) is minimal.

If we are convinced that 36 inches of deposit had accumulated in place one layer at a time and was in fact undisturbed, perhaps we would have to consider a span of several hundred or more years to account for the depth and nature of the deposition. Unfortunately, no such undisturbed development seems likely, and there are other factors which need to be introduced. The first is that we know from ethnographic accounts that a number of ritual activities were carried out on the village premises that involved the digging of pits and trenches. This is in addition to secular features such as fire pits, roasting ovens and possible house pits, all involving the movement of the deposit. This means that the midden at any of the main village sites has been churned and turned over perhaps several times during the course of its accumulation. At Molpa the vast majority of the pottery was recovered in the first 18 to 24 inches of the deposit, with occasional sherds turning up as deep as 48 inches. The deeper specimens can be accounted for by rodent activities and present no real problem. The majority of the sherds found more than 12 but less than 30 inches deep could easily have been the result of the churning and mixing described above. This suggests that the whole 36 inches of proposed average San Luis Rey deposit need not have been developed during the time that pottery was actually in use in the area.

Another important point which bears on this problem is that ceramics are not part of the basic Luiseño cultural pattern as this is defined in the mythology. In the creation myth, for example, where all important elements of Luiseño (San Luis Rey) culture are enumerated, no mention is made of pottery. Pottery does not seem to be of the elements born of the earth mother, nor is it a significant element in any of the ritual. Even recognizing the conservative nature of Luiseño religion it seems likely that if pottery had been part of the life way for any significant time, it would have been incorporated into the ritual — into some of the songs — and even into the creation myth in some way or another. In contrast, the Diegueno ritual and mythology do include references to pottery, and pottery was commonly used in ritual activities.

To assume a position consistent with the **data** as
they are now conceived, we suggest that some pottery
probably filtered across from Diegueno territory perhaps as early as A.D. 1200-1300 under some circumstances,
but that the introduction of pottery as a regular and
important element in the San Luis Rey life way probably
did not take place until a century or two before the
arrival of the Spanish (perhaps A.D. 1500-1600).

CULTURE CHANGE

Although stratigraphic sequencing of cultural phases
is not demonstrated firmly at Molpa, a comparative analysis of the Molpa collection and the preceramic collection from SD-132 does provide information on change
through time. In the initial discussion of the sequence
between the phases designated San Luis Rey I and San
Luis Rey II, all that could be said about the latter was
that it was made up of the San Luis Rey I assemblage
with the addition of pottery. Now that we have described
in more detail what is present in San Luis Rey II, it
is possible to discriminate somewhat more in the way of
cultural change as this phase developed.

First, it must be recognized that the addition of
pottery may well have brought with it other new elements.
While the addition of ceramic cooking containers to the
artifact inventory may not have been of great cultural
significance, other artifacts, and presumably other new
ideas, came into the San Luis Rey drainage along with
pottery. Among these are pipes and figurines.

Pipes have not yet been recovered from the San Luis
Rey I assemblages, although tubular pipes are ancient
in California and stone pipes are prominent in some
versions of the Luiseño creation myth. Ethnographic
sources suggest a tubular clay pipe for the Luiseño
(Rogers 1936: 50), but these have not yet been reported
for the area from any archaeological context. In any
event, the introduction of ceramic pipes of a new form
(the Diegueño bow-shaped pipe) appears to be of the
changes that took place with the beginning of the San
Luis Rey II phase. Because of the importance of

tobacco and smoking to California groups, and the ritual contexts of such activity, we may suspect that something more is involved here than mere transmission of an item of material culture. At present, this problem can only be indicated as something worth further study.

Also of particular interest is the occurrence for the first time in San Luis Rey II contexts of pottery figurines, sometimes formed over a seed or acorn. While baked-clay figurines are known in central California from sites containing no pottery, such pre-pottery figurines are not known in southern California, and there is so far no evidence of figurines in San Luis Rey I or any other preceramic assemblage in southern California. As with pipes, pottery figurines have a ritual or symbolic significance that may well go beyond the mere introduction of a material trait, particularly in this case where the figurines are associated with a major food resource, the acorn.

Hence, in saying that San Luis Rey II represents the addition of pottery to a basic culture already present in the area, it must be remembered that "pottery" includes in this case a distinctive kind of pipe and an unusual kind of figurine. Another element which may be related to the shift from San Luis Rey I to San Luis Rey II is the probable addition of painted pictographs to the San Luis Rey II cultural assemblage. We have no way of dating the introduction of this practice into the area, but it may be significant that all known San Luis Rey II sites either have pictographs on the site proper, or have an outlying pictograph rock which can be associated directly with the site. In most cases the association between the outlying painted rock and the village can be documented ethnographically. In others the location is consistent and agrees with ethnographically based expectations. Many of the sites here are multi-component with San Luis Rey I deposits underlying those of the San Luis Rey II deposits. In such cases we have no way of tying the painted features to one component to the exclusion of the other. Nevertheless, it is worth noting that none of the "pure" San Luis Rey I sites so far investigated has any evidence of rock painting. There is some evidence suggesting that the earlier milling-stone (Pauma) people may have made pecked petroglyph designs of an entirely different nature. These "pecked" elements are quite rare, and little is known of their affiliation. None has been reported in association with San Luis Rey complex sites, and of the several hundred known "Pauma" occupation sites in this area, none can be connected directly with any of the painted elements. In sum, it is possible to say that (1) the earlier milling-stone occupancy probably included occasional pecked designs in their assemblage of cultural traits; (2) none of these pecked elements has been tied to any of the later San Luis Rey sites; (3) painted designs are clearly part of the San Luis Rey II assemblage; (4) evidence so far in hand does not support the presence of either the painted elements or the pecked elements in the San Luis Rey I phase; and (5) the pecked design elements are stylistically different from those typical of the painted designs and no relationships are suggested.

The cup-shaped depressions may also coincide with the shift from San Luis Rey I to San Luis Rey II. These elements, while not common, are known from several sites over a considerable part of upland San Diego County. At present, there is no way to date them, but there is some indirect evidence suggesting an affiliation with the earlier rather than the later phase of the San Luis Rey occupancy. This evidence may be outlined as follows: (1) there is no mention of these elements in the ethnographic literature; (2) they were not mentioned by Luiseño informants working this project at the time Molpa was excavated; (3) painted pictographs and most other features found associated with San Luis Rey II sites are discussed in the literature or can be explained by surviving Luiseño informants; (4) similar elements in other parts of California are said to be "earlier" forms of petroglyphs (Baumhoff 1969, personal communication); (5) there appears to be some differential weathering between these elements and other grinding or wear surfaces in similar bedrock outcroppings on the same sites. Lichen growth, moss, and general surface characteristics of the rock itself all point to some time differences here. We are aware that this is not definitive evidence of a time difference in its own right, but it should be considered in conjunction with other indirect evidence all of which supports the notion that these elements may predate the most recent San Luis Rey occupancy of these sites.

Other kinds of cultural change may be indicated in the artifacts, particularly the points of which we have a fairly large sample of complete specimens. A careful comparison was made to see whether the San Luis Rey II points from Molpa differ in any way from the points associated with the preceramic site SD-132. The results (table 6) are interesting; although the two sites have the same forms (types) of points, made of the same materials, the points from the later site (Molpa) are smaller and lighter than those from the earlier site. This is not something that is visible without careful measurement, and of course it can only be determined with a sample of some size, but it is significant to note that even within the late time period, points were being made smaller and smaller with the passage of time, the smallest points being associated with protohistoric and historic sites. The magnitude of the change was certainly too small to be observable to the makers of the points, and it is therefore an unconscious but consistent directional change.

To summarize, point lengths became shorter by an average of 5 mm. between the time of SD-132 and Molpa; this change was accompanied by expectable decreases in point width and point weight. There appears to be no functional explanation for this size change, which is too small to have any adaptive value. However, the shift may indicate a slightly better control of the stone-flaking process since many of the points are of crystalline quartz, which is very difficult to chip into small forms.

Unfortunately, for reasons previously stated we do not know the magnitude of the time differences between the two sites and cannot estimate the rate at which points were decreasing in size. The best guess would be that the sites are separated in time by a few hundred years. If the size change was at a more or less constant rate, it indicates that point lengths in this region were getting shorter by less than a millimeter per century. This comparison also suggests that it ought to be possible to seriate sites in the San Luis

TABLE 8

Comparison of Point Size, Molpa and SDi-132

	Length (mm.)	Width (mm.)	Thickness (mm.)	Weight (gms.)
MOLPA N = 20	R: 13.4-26.7 Av: 19.6	R: 9.8-19.6 Av: 13.3	R: 2.6-4.6 Av: 3.48	R: 0.3-1.2 Av: 0.655
SD-132 N = 12	R: 19.1-38.0 Av: 25.0	R: 11.1-24.5 Av: 16.4	R: 2.9-8.9 Av: 5.10	R: 0.0-4.5 Av: 1.491

Meighan (1954) gives the average point length for SD-132 as 23 mm. This number was derived from a total sample with many points having the tips missing and the overall length estimated. For the present table, more careful control of the measurements results in a smaller sample; only two of the twelve points used have any part missing, and they are sufficiently complete so that their length can be estimated to within a millimeter or so.

The same paper refers to a sample of points from a known Luiseno village of historic period (SDi-616, Taghanashpa), which have an average length of 20 mm. This is very close to the average for the historic site of Molpa.

Of the twelve specimens, five have very small flakes missing so their original weight is a trace higher than recorded. Eliminating the one heavy point (4.5 α.) changes the average point weight to 1.21 grams, which is probably closer to the true average for San Luis Rey I points.

Rey River drainage on the basis of average point size and to recognize differences in time of 500 to 1000 years. Such a sequencing of sites is not yet possible because the sample of entire points is too small for most sites. Also, the careful measurements needed have not yet been made for most collections including those published so far.

Finally, as another change between San Luis Rey I and San Luis Rey II, it may be suggested that the variety and specialization of grinding implements increased somewhat during San Luis Rey II times. This must remain a suggestion because of the heavy reliance on bedrock grinding implements which are impossible to assign to a specific cultural phase. However, as a possibility for future study, it may be suggested that San Luis Rey II saw the introduction of the basketry hopper mortar and possibly other variations in grinding implements. Since grinding tools are the basic food-preparation devices for California Indians, the grinding tool assemblage has important implications for the adaptive efficiency of San Luis Rey Indians to their environment.

It is concluded that San Luis Rey II is considerably more than "San Luis Rey I plus pottery". Even though the region continued to be occupied by the "same" people with the "same" material culture, many subtle but significant cultural changes were taking place. When these are worked out in detail, it will be possible to say quite a bit about cultural process within a basic hunting-gathering stratum. Needless to say, such definition is impossible without meticulous excavation and meticulous description of site collection; in the absence of more detailed site reports forour region, we can barely begin to suggest and document significant changes.

4. INTERPRETATIONS AND EVALUATIONS

By use of archaeological and ethnohistoric data, we have presented a definition of the content and distribution of the San Luis Rey archaeological complex. Our knowledge is still limited by many gaps in the available information, but enough is known to allow some suggestion of the broader implications of our study. Any new research provides a test of some of the formulations and conclusions expressed by archaeologists, and it is appropriate to examine our materials to see how they conform to current ideas and issues in archaeology.

SETTLEMENT PATTERNS

First, with regard to settlement pattern, the bipolar seasonal camps described as typical of the San Luis Rey area cannot be fitted into existing classifications such as that devised by Beardsley et al, (1956). The San Luis Rey settlement pattern is clearly not a Central Based Wandering pattern, nor is it Semi-Permanent Sedentary as this pattern is defined. There is, for example, no evidence of periodic changing of village locations for any of the reasons cited by Beardsley et al. For all practical purposes, the San Luis Rey peoples were sedentary and lived in permanent villages. They had most of the attributes of a sedentary agricultural subsistence but lacked agriculture itself. The high productivity of the oak groves in each territory, plus a wide range of supplementary food resources combined with a simple storage technology made it possible to subsist on a level that in other contexts would be considered formative as this concept is defined by Willey and Phillips (1958) (See also Meighan, 1959b: 305 for discussion of the concept of a formative stage in California archaeology.)

RELIGIOUS ARTIFACTS AND THEIR RECOGNITION

This subsistence was achieved with a relatively simple technology and the tool kit recovered archaeologically does not reflect the culture complexity expected for largely sedentary peoples. The range and variety of tools recovered is more like one would expect to find in a somewhat less complex and more mobile Great Basin group. In contrast to expectations based on archaeologically recovered tool kits, ethnographic data describe a rather elaborate and complex round of ritual activities and a great deal of social interaction related in various ways to these ceremonies. Except for pictographs which are usually confined to crude and simple geometric forms, there is very little indication of this religious complexity in the archaeological record. Charmstones or similar elements associated with religious activities in other areas are not part of the San Luis Rey inventory, and decorated elements, be they ceramic or worked stone, are conspicuous by their absence. Shell inlay work such as that found in the Chumash territory to the north and to a lesser degree in Diegueno territory to the south has not been found in San Luis Rey collections. Only three artifacts definitely identified as having ritual significance are likely to be recovered archaeologically, and in two instances their significance would not be recognized from the archaeology alone (the small mortar used for the Toloache ceremony, the pestles used to pound the Datura root, and a small chipped stone element identified as the insert from a ceremonial wand). Figurines may have had some ritual significance, but are crude and poorly developed at best. A number of other ritual items are known ethnographically that would not survive to be recovered archaeologically (feather elements, simple textiles, and baskets). However, even considering the full range of elements recognized as part of the religious life, using both ethnographic and archaeological resources, the number of material elements seem pitifully small. This same lack of concern with material wealth or technical elaboration seems to carry over to ornamentation. Beads and pendants, common in

adjacent areas for the same period of time, are quite
rare. As mentioned earlier, this may be due in part to
the nature of the cremation practices which make no
attempt to gather the ashes or burned offerings after
the burning. This can be only a partial explanation,
however, and it seems necessary to conclude that the use
of beads and ornamentation was minimal in the San Luis
Rey territory. In general then, it is possible to say
that the San Luis Rey material culture inventory was
simple and confined to a few basic forms. This is in
contrast with ethnographic information which documents
a rich, varied, and reasonably complex cultural situation
for the same people.

There are several artifacts in the Molpa inventory,
for example, which would have been misinterpreted completely had specific ethnographic information not been
available. The ceremonial wand insert (pl. 8, g) would
have been classified as some kind of projectile point
or small cutting tool. It would have been recognized as
intrusive, or deviant in form and different from the
other "knives", but there would have been no way to
associate this artifact with any ritual activity. There
is nothing inherent in the artifact suggesting such relationships, and there was nothing in the context which
could tie it to a specific activity. Knowing what we
do about Luiseño religious practices and disposition of
the ceremonial artifacts themselves, it is possible to
suggest, in fact, that the <u>recovery</u> of this element was
entirely fortuitous and that its disposition in the midden was random, and not part of any activity "pattern"
which might be reflected in the spatial disposition of
artifacts recovered in archaeological contexts. Further,
artifacts making up the "bundle" of the religious chief
(nota) were passed from generation to generation. Some
elements made of perishable material may have been replaced from time to time, but there was no occasion to
incorporate any of the elements into the site except by
rarest of accidents. For the most part, these were
sacred and dangerous items. They were not casually utilized or thrown about. They were <u>not</u> cremated with their
owners as were other belongings, and so would not be
found in a mortuary context. Except by accident in fact
such elements would <u>never</u> be part of an archaeological

context even if preservation were not a factor and even if every element had a tag attached explaining its use. It is possible that in the course of a dance (often performed at night) the stone insert placed in the end of the chief's sacred wand could become loosened and fall out. It is possible that because of the nature of the dancing surface and the heavy traffic there, the insert might not be found and would thusly be incorporated into the midden. However, the <u>association</u> of this stone artifact with the dance area (wamkish?) would probably not be recognized archaeologically. The wamkish itself is such a simple structure it is unlikely that it could be recognized archaeologically (none have been so far). Assuming that one might recognize a ceremonial dance floor archaeologically in the Luiseño (San Luis Rey) territory, there is still no basis for recognizing the insert stone as a ceremonial item (based on its own attributes). Further, there is no evidence to suggest that the associated artifacts found in the wamkish area would be separable from those typical of some other activity area within the village. Ritual activities were carried on at several loci over the site proper depending on the kind of ceremonial being carried out. With the exception of features such as stone-lined pits, which might be discovered archaeologically, (assuming they were not destroyed as part of the ritual itself) most of the elements associated with these ceremonials were either perishable, lacking in specific identification or were passed from generation to generation with little chance that they would become part of the archaeological deposit. This applies not only to the nota's bundle, but to the ceremonial mortar, ceremonial wand, and indeed all known ritual items.

In numerous archaeological contexts all over southern California spirelopped (spire-ground) <u>Olivella</u> shells are identified as beads. Without a doubt many were beads or used as ornaments of one kind or another. This is a logical interpreation of this element, and there is nothing in the archaeology to refute it. Similar artifacts are part of the San Luis Rey inventory. Here, however, at least some of these "beads" were used to make teeth for figures used in an image-burning ceremony. The possibility that this usage would be recognizable from the archaeology is virtually nil. Archaeologically then, there is nothing to suggest even the existence of the imageburning ceremony, let alone the nature of the associated artifacts. There is nothing which would permit any specific interpretation for these artifacts short of the preservation of portions of the image with the face intact. This is highly unlikely given the perishable nature of the image, and the fact that the ritual itself called for the complete destruction of the figure. Under normal circumstances there is no way that such a figure could survive intact, and in prehistoric contexts presumably no reason to want one to survive, since this would be an indication of careless handling of important ritual activities, and thus very dangerous.

IMPLICATIONS OF THE ETHNOHISTORY FOR "ADAPTIVE" EXPLANATIONS OF CULTURAL CHANGE

The preceding discussion has a bearing on important theoretical issues because it emphasizes the contrast between the intellectual objectives of archaeology and the possibilities for attainment of those objectives. It is nothing new to point out the limitations of archaeological interpretation, but our case example is an additional caution to those who believe that archaeological evidence can provide the basis for laws of human development. In contrasting what we know ethnohistorically from what we can discover from archaeological evidence only, it is clear that as archaeologists we would fail to recognize or correctly interpret a major segment, perhaps the most important segment, of the life-way of the people we are studying. If we ignore the richness of ritual and religion, we are left with what we can describe, thereby unwittingly overstressing direct environmental adaptation as reflected in the archaeological food remains and artifacts for procuring and processing food. Hence we may be led, as some contemporary archaeologists seem to be, to the view that ecology is solely explanatory of human development and that all change can be explained in terms of adaptive response to situations which are ultimately environmental in nature. We feel strongly that it is not enough simply

to acknowledge there are differences in inventories between living cultures and archaeological assemblages; it
is essential that the effects these differences might
have in any archaeological interpretation be fully understood. We may never be able to know what ramifications the missing evidence might have with regard to
our interpretive efforts, but some room for alternative
possibilities must be provided and some recognition of
influences other than those obviously present in the
archaeological inventory must be made.

Not many archaeological studies can refer directly
to historic or ethnographic documentation to fill out
the meager bits and pieces taken from the excavation
units. Mostly, archaeologists must work with indirect
analogy in one form or another, or use other sources of
interpretative data such as experimentation, special
studies designed to document artifact function, and
artifact relationships in conjunction with some kind of
indirect analogy. Sometimes there is little more to lean
on than simple logic. These are all important and useful
sources of information, and they are improving constantly as archaeologists practice greater and greater precision in their recovery techniques and utilize more
sophisticated methods. None, however, provide the
wherewithall to make decisions about (1) the specific
alternate possibilities which might be overlooked because of missing data, (2) data which are present but
which have been misinterpreted, or (3) data which are
present but which have no meaning. None of the available sources of interpretative information outside of
the direct historical approach permit the archaeologists to say much about possible meaning. None provide
the basis for discussing behavior where there are no
surviving artifacts reflecting that behavior. Those
who believe archaeology is a science, the primary goal
of which is to elucidate laws of human development, cannot stand the uncertainty inherent in archaeological
data and attempt to reduce or eliminate these problems.
As mentioned above, the easy reductionistic argument is
to assume that all human behavior is explainable in terms
of response to environmental challenges, and to seek in
the environment "explanations" for all cultural manifestations present in the archaeology. If explanation

for the meaning of objects cannot be found, no matter when enough is known it will become clear that there is an environmental explanation for whatever puzzles us. We must reject this line of thought as an oversimplification which cannot be applied even to the culture history of hunters and gatherers like the Luiseño, who had an unquestionably close relationship with their environmental resources. Even the Luiseño did not live by bread alone, and the ethnography makes abundantly clear that what was really important to them was not seed-gathering but a complex and rich religious and philosophical structure. However limited we may be at getting at this aspect of life from our archaeological evidence, we cannot assume that we have understood or explained the archaeology until we have sought the humanist component of San Luis Rey life as well as the social and environmental aspects of it.

We agree that adaptation is critical. We agree that this "adaptive" approach may be basic to understanding many prehistoric situations. As an application of this thinking we agree that much of the ethnographically described Luiseño (San Luis Rey) pattern, including the ritual activities may have been adaptive and functioned as a resource distribution mechanism for the area at large. However, the point here is (1) there are other things that can contribute to a cultural configuration besides adaptive responses to environmental resources; and (2) often these other things will not be recognized in an archaeological context when direct ethnographic sources of information cannot be utilized. How much of the ritual of the San Luis Rey complex, for example, would be recovered from the archaeology of this region regardless of the recovery methods used or the philosophical bent of the archaeologist, and how much of this ritual could be seen as adaptive under the circumstances? Probably none. This in spite of the fact that we would have some of the ritual elements in hand but simply would be at a loss to explain them. There is no way to know from the archaeology that officiating participants in ceremonial activities must be paid. There would be nothing in the archaeology suggesting that these are obligatory responsibilities, and that they are reciprocal in nature. We would find the pictographs suggesting a ritual of some kind, but we could not—on the basis of archaeological data alone—relate them to any specific ceremonial activity. Under certain extremely fortuitous circumstances one might find an association of artifacts that would imply some religious or ceremonial activity. However, there are many more situations where no such associations are found. Are we to infer from these archaeological deficiencies that there were no ceremonial activities? Or that they existed but had no influence on the culture pattern or life-way? All of this is known to all archaeologists. However, the difference between the archaeologically recovered San Luis Rey II inventory and the inventory of the ethnographically described Luiseño provoked some discussion of the kinds of interpretative problems one might encounter, and in light of recent works which tend to disregard the possible effects of these internal factors, the implications inherent in these examples for archaeological interpretations in other contexts are worth discussion.

Most anthropologists recognize that socio-religious activities represent the most difficult aspects of culture to recover archaeologically. Thus the complications mentioned above would not be unexpected. On the other hand, the area where archaeologists seem best able to make useful contributions lies with the recognition and interpretation of settlement patterns and discussion of basic subsistence. Current thinking would have these discussions of subsistence and settlement patterns tied to some direct adaptive response—and would see the basis for whatever change might be recognized as a response to this adaptation (Binford 1964: 440, 1968; Kushner 1970: 126-130). Looking at both the ethnographic and archaeological evidence from this area, several questions might be raised regarding the potential for relating changes in the basic San Luis Rey cultural pattern directly to some adaptive response to the physical environment. There is little difficulty in seeing the overall San Luis Rey pattern as an adaptive response to a set of environmental conditions. The problem here is, can we talk about this adaptation on the basis of archaeological evidence alone? And further can we talk about it in specific terms or are we restricted to the general

observations that are by now truisms about hunters and
gatherers? What kinds of specific problems would have
to be resolved if archaeologists were to talk about San
Luis Rey Settlement patterns, basic subsistence, and
life-ways in terms of some kind of adaptive response to
physical environment. One such problem specific to the
San Luis Rey situation is suggested below:

The distribution of archaeological sites within the
San Luis Rey territorial boundaries include major villages, ceremonial sites, and presumably small hunting
or gathering stations of one kind or another. The vast
majority of the latter are identified by some kind of
milling element (bedrock mortar or milling-stone or
both), a smear of slightly discolored soil in the vicinity of said milling-stone element, and occasionally
a few fragmentary artifacts or chipping waste suggesting some kind of cultural activity other than seed-
processing. With respect to the artifactual evidence
found on these sites it can be stated almost without
reservation that few if any diagnostic forms will be
present and only on the rarest of occasions will potsherds, projectile points, knives, beads, or other
"usable" forms be recovered. Thus for every site with
a "recognizable" diagnostic artifact inventory, there
will be as many as a dozen or more of these "stations"
with few or no artifacts. At the present time these
sites are seen as satellite hunting and gathering locations, contemporary to and belonging with the San Luis
Rey pattern. Before this can be stated with any cer-
tainty, however, these postulated relationships must be
supported with empirical data. Basically there is little
question but that these stations are in fact part of the
San Luis Rey pattern. However, the question is <u>which</u>
phase of the San Luis Rey pattern? And more importantly,
what changes have taken place in these relationships
through time? Step one in the resolution of this problem would be definitive dating of the various satellite
stations. This would mean that nearly every one of
these stations would have to be dated. Dating one site
or three would be useful and important but would not
answer the question being raised here, and the likeli-
hood of recovering datable material in a reliable
meaningful context for sites in this category is very

low. Nevertheless, unless we can establish the relative contemporaneity of <u>each</u> of these stations with one or both of the proposed San Luis Rey phases, future comments about settlement patterns, subsistence, etc. may well be distorted. How <u>many</u> of the stations extant in the San Luis Rey territory can be associated with San Luis Rey I, as opposed to San Luis Rey II? Knowing this could be important and could suggest a shift in the utilization of some resources in this area during San Luis Rey times. Another possibility which has to be considered at this point is that these small scattered stations represent the earliest San Luis Rey occupancy of this region followed by several centuries or millennia of gradual consolidation or agglutination into larger and larger groups, and in time to establish villages all in response to a settling-in process resulting from more and more knowledge of the local environmental resources. Again resolution of this possibility would call for in addition to other data sources detailed control of the time factors for all sites within the area.

A problem related to the identification of the satellite stations is archaeological recognition of the seasonal round as a basis for San Luis Rey subsistence. Given the distribution of major sites and some knowledge of transhumance practices elsewhere in the world, such a round might be logically indicated. The point is that lacking ethnographic information, there is no obvious empirical evidence in the archaeology itself that would point to this kind of subsistence. There is nothing available in the evidence that would identify the mountain site of Jaculi as the summer village of the settlement at La Jolla or Japicha. Looking at the overall distribution of sites in the area one could just as well suggest the existence of mountain people, foothill people, and valley people, and never see the possibility for a vertical distribution cross-cutting these ecological zones. On the other hand there are some <u>potential</u> data sources which might indicate the relationships between the lowland and upland villages. The ties in this case would be tenuous and the data difficult if not impossible to recover. The initial step in this direction would be the identification of sites in both lowland

and upland contexts as part of the same cultural pattern. This is fairly easy and has been done already. The second step would call for establishing that the villages in the two zones were contemporary. In the case of the present study this time relationship was established ethnographically. Under the circumstances it would be a great deal more difficult to document such a relationship in prehistoric times, other than on logical grounds based on extrapolation from historic data. If both of the above conditions prevailed (the villages were part of the same cultural pattern and were contemporary in time), a hypothesis could be formulated calling for seasonal occupancy of the two basic environmental zones. Using ethnographic sources (both general and specific), logic, and information from other archaeological contexts, several possible data sources to document this relationship might be predicted:

1. Differences in food remains in the two locales. Recovery of this category of data would depend on preservation of organic remains in one form or another, and possibly on artifactual evidence for differential resource exploitation.

2. Because of markedly different climatic circumstances in the two locales, one might predict differences in house forms or mode of construction (surface units versus houses in pits, etc.).

3. There could well be a differential distribution of features reflecting different kinds of non-subsistence activities in each of the two zones (ritual performed in one area but not the other for one reason or another).

Given our general knowledge of ethnographic data for California at large, these differences (and perhaps several more) might be predicted for the San Luis Rey situation in prehistoric times. Given recent advances in recovery techniques it would appear that correct archaeological identification of these circumstances would not seem especially difficult. On the other hand examination of the situation as we know it to be (again based on ethnographic data sources) suggests that these goals are in fact nearly impossible ones, and that they could be accomplished only with rare luck and the fortuitous

preservation of perishable elements. Plant food differences did exist between the two areas, but for these
to be significant they would first have to be recovered
from the deposit (a highly unlikely situation); generic
or in some cases species identification would have to
be made to establish the differences empirically, and it
would be necessary to quantify these remains if we want-
ed to demonstrate that plant species A was the key food
source in the lowland contexts, and plant food B the
prime resource in the upland context. Finding examples
of each plant in the middens of each of the sites without quantitative differences simply means that the resources were there: it tells us nothing about their
importance to the people. Seasonal differences in time
of maturation of some staple item, such as the acorn,
might logically suggest the indicated pattern, but this
is not the same as demonstrating it from the archaeology
alone. The key artifact associated with this staple
item is the bedrock mortar and upland mortars are identical to lowland mortars. Acorns from Quercus kellogii
are processed exactly the same as acorns from Quercus
dumosa. There are important plant resources found on
upland contexts that were not normally found in the
lower elevations, and we might be able to identify remains of these seeds in the midden (under unusual circumstances) but since storage of resources was practiced
in the area, simply finding one kind of plant remains in
either of the two site situations tells us very little
about the subsistence round itself. Mountain acorns
and presumably other seed resources were carried to lowland villages and stored for winter use. The reverse
was not the case, however, and seemingly no lowland
resources were carried into the upland sites in any
quantity. Thus documentation of upland seed resources
in the lowland sites might be used to suggest some kind
of relationship. It could have just as well been trade
as seasonal migration, however, and there seems to be no
obvious way to separate the two possibilities archaeologically.

A similar complication would prevail with regard to
animal food resources. Deer were important during the
summer and fall seasons in the upland contexts. However,
the climate is such that there is no marked seasonal

migration of deer, and they could be taken as well during
the winter encampments in the lowland situations. Thus
while a few more deer might be taken during the summer
in the mountain contexts than in the winter camp locales,
in general, deer remains would be present in both situations. The chances of recognizing these differences
quantitatively are slim. For one thing, evidence from
the sites so far excavated suggests that deer bone is
not commonly present in the midden deposits. All the
ethnographic evidence indicates considerable emphasis
on deer hunting, but this is not reflected in the refuse.
Thus some other variable has to be introduced. There
may have been some cultural practice, not described
ethnographically, which caused the bone to be scattered
or destroyed. (Dogs may have contributed to the scatter
and removal of bone outside the midden area itself.)
In any case and for whatever reasons, the archaeological
record here is unlikely to include recognizable differences in faunal material in the two seasonal campsite
situations, and even less likely to produce evidence
documenting the seasonality of the occupancy and the
importance of the seasonal round.

The possibility that different hunting patterns,
recovery of different kinds of resources (or whatever)
would be reflected in artifact differences also must be
considered. Archaeologists traditionally have talked
a lot about hunting camps and other special activity
sites of one kind or another. More recently this concern has intensified and considerable effort is being
invested in attempts to isolate "tool kits" associated
with special activities. In some contexts, at least,
this recognition of tool kits seem feasible, and the
possibility exists that these special aggregates of artifacts may in fact reflect some kind of seasonal activities within the overall subsistence pattern. Recent
work by Thomas (1971) seems to fall into this category.
In this case, there is recognition of seasonal patterns
in terms of artifact differences located in different
and separable environmental zones, which are tied to
computer-based predictions made on the basis of an
ethnographic data input. Hopefully the application of
this rigorous methodology to the San Diego County material would produce similar results. This is considered

unlikely, however, for several reasons. Investigations
so far have revealed no differences in artifacts qual-
itatively or quantitatively) between the two village
situations. Because the size of the territory involved
for each settlement (winter and summer village complex)
is relatively small, there is little occasion for extended foraging or hunting trips. Overnight stays may
have been the exception rather than the rule. Thus the
production of tools and the resulting chipping waste
would most likely have been made at the base camps. The
chance of identifying a special activity camp associated
with deer hunting, for example, is almost nonexistent.
Further, such a deer-hunting camp assuming that one
might exist, would not necessarily have the connotation
of seasonal use that might be implied in some other environmental contexts. Similar large animals (mainly
deer) were hunted with similar (identical?) tools in
both the summer and winter camp situations. The artifacts then, like the faunal materials discussed above,
are not likely to help in the recognition of the upland-
lowland relationships associated with a seasonal round.

House structures are known from the ethnography to
be different in the two locales. This is hard to document archaeologically since structures and house floors
have not yet been encountered in the archaeological deposits. Even if they were recoverable, however, all this
would do is confirm that the same pattern prevailed in
prehistoric times. It would not tell us anything about
relationships between upland and lowland villages and
would not lead to any recognition of the seasonal round
as the basis for the extant settlement pattern.

A third possibility for recognition of upland-
lowland differences depends on the recognition of different sets of nonsubsistence-based activities in the
two locales.

It would appear that most ritual activities took
place in the winter village location. (Pictographs,
for example, are found only associated with winter villages.) If this is the case then the wamkish should be
found only at the winter villages and not on the mountain. The same would apply to stone-lined pits used
in the girl's puberty ceremonials, and the special huts
made for the Toloache ceremony, or the pits used in the

Wana-wut ritual. These kinds of distinctions could be important in the identification of the mountain villages as part of a more complex pattern, rather than as independent entities. The problem is that they have not yet been identified archaeologically, and there are reasons why they may never be so identified. On the other hand, the location and identification of such features should be part of the long term goals of any research in this region.

We see the San Luis Rey Complex as an end product of a long settling-in process and as such, adaptation to the physical environment is recognized as of great import. On the other hand, it appears from the available data that there is little basis for suggesting this environmental context as the explanation for important aspects of the life-way itself. Much of the San Luis Rey pattern was of course conditioned by the environment. The adoption of the seasonal round permitted the most efficient utilization of resources within a limited area. Several key elements in the San Luis Rey inventory reflect basic hunter-gatherer subsistence practices and thus aspects of the environment. There is, however, substantial evidence in the pattern suggesting that the basic San Luis Rey life-way and subsequent changes in this life style through a millennium or more of time, were influenced as much by traditional factors as they were by external (noncultural) forces. To suggest that only one set of influences was operative here would be naive, and in this case at least, it would appear that there is convincing evidence for the influence of ideational or traditional forces acting upon the manner in which the suggested adaptation was effected.

To further emphasize this point, comparisons can be made with the contemporary Cuyamaca cultural pattern in the adjacent Diegueño territory. Here adaptation to an identical upland environment has produced a similar subsistence base as would be expected, but with a recognizably different life style and artifactual inventory. If adaptation to environment is the key factor determining the nature of any cultural pattern to the exclusion of ideational factors (tradition) how can we account for these differences in life style, world view, and general cultural pattern?

If tradition and diffusion of items and ideas are not critical factors in the shaping of this cultural pattern, some other basis must be sought that will explain the rather clear-cut Colorado River and Hohokam-like characteristics found in the Cuyamaca cultural inventory. It does not make sense to suggest that the mountain peoples of San Diego County south of Lake Henshaw developed these characteristics as part of an adaptive response to their environment, when the Hohokam environment is entirely different with few if any shared attributes. It is even less sensible to suggest that the Cuyamaca peoples developed this pattern in response to environmental influences, but that the San Luis Rey people next door, in an identical environment, failed to get the message and developed an aberrant pattern in spite of the environmental influences. If external (environmental) factors were critical in these two developments, it is important to know what was going on that set the two apart. What environmental influences for example triggered the shift from burial to cremation in the mortuary practices some three to five millennia ago? Both groups practice cremation and have done so for some time, but one area (Cuyamaca) represents the end product of a long development in place, while the other area has cremation as part of an intrusive complex presumably unrelated to the basic milling-stone occupancy found in this area some 5000 years ago. We are most interested in seeing how these two patterns could in fact be the byproduct of direct responses to the same environment, and future work in this area will be directed toward such an understanding. For the present, however, it seems necessary to reiterate at least part of the traditional dogma and propose that what we see with the San Luis Rey complex is the end product of a distinct cultural tradition modified by adaptations to a new environmental milieu and influenced by diffused ideas from the south and east during the thousand or more years of its settling-in process. The adjacent Cuyamaca complex (in an identical environmental locale) likewise was the end product of a distinct cultural tradition which developed in place out of a milling-stone base, modified en route by important influences from the Colorado River region (diffusion of ideas). That there may be an environmental basis for this contact and diffusion (periodic filling of the Blake Sea with fresh water) is not disputed in the case of the Cuyamaca people. But the changes themselves were not adaptive in terms of this recurring resource, and the movement of the mountain peoples to the shores of this lake from time to time simply set up the contacts with adjacent Colorado-basin peoples. The concept of urn burial of cremated remains and its associated belief system a hallmark of the Cuyamaca complex, the Colorado River peoples, and the Hohokam seems in no way a response to the rise and fall of the Blake Sea.

PROSPECTS FOR THE FUTURE

While the tone of the preceding discussion has been somewhat pessimistic because of our frustration in dealing with specific interpretative problems, our aim is constructive and our hopes for the long-range future of archaeological investigations are definitely optimistic. To stress the difficulties of archaeological interpretation, and to insist that general statements about cultural development are premature, is not to say that the game isn't worth the candle, nor that nothing useful can be learned even from such limited investigations as that reported here. In fact, we know a great deal more in the way of historical facts from our studies, and the questions we raise, both substantive and theoretical, point the way to better investigative procedures and more secure answers.

There are now hundreds of archaeological sites known in the region of our investigation. Few of them will yield much in the way of archaeological collections, but any may contribute to the history of the region. The knowledge to be gained however, still depends to a large extent on traditional methods of archaeological survey and excavation. Close attention to the ethnography and ethnohistory of the area will provide some basis for improved interpretation of the objects found, and even some reconstruction of the objects not found but yet present in the archaeological culture. Out of

this can come, not a series of laws about human development, but a realistic portrayal of a life-way now
extinct —an essential precondition to the formulation of
general statements about hunters and gatherers, or about
the multiple ways in which man has ordered his life on
earth.

ACKNOWLEDGEMENTS AND END NOTES

We would like to thank the many Luiseño Indians
from Pauma, Rincon, Potrero, and La Jolla who made important contributions to these papers. Max Peters, Max
Calac, Herman Calac, and Ray Pachito from Pauma all
helped with place names and plant material indentifi-
cation. Mr. Henry Rodriguez from Potrero (Cuca) is the
acknowledged local specialist on Luiseño ethnobotany,
and much of the plant material information included here
must be credited to his pioneer efforts. Mr. Romulo
Sobenish from La Jolla (Japicha?) helped with place
names on Palomar Mountain and in the Potrero-La Jolla
regions. Herman Calac from Tecolote and Thurmand
McCormic from Rincon provided invaluable insights and
information on the Luiseño life-way in general, and on
the village of Molpa in particular. Mr. Pachito is a
nota (priest) from the village of Pauma and much of what
can be said about Luiseño religion and settlement patterns can in some way or another be traced back to his
knowledge.
We would also like to thank Dr. William Harrison
who turned over his field notes and records on Molpa to
us so that the report could be completed. Mr. Manchester
Boddy (now deceased) was most generous at the time of
the excavations. He gave us permission to excavate the
site and helped in many other ways. Mr. F. D.
Fitzsimmons acting as agent for this property assisted
with the remapping and new studies instigated during the
summer of 1968.
Many more kinds of artifacts were recovered from
SDi-535 than are indicated on table 7 in appendix A.
Over the years some of these have been misplaced and
many more are in the hands of private collectors. Thus
they are not available for restudy or quantification.

APPENDIX A. ARCHAEOLOGICAL RESOURCES OF PALOMAR MOUNTAIN STATE PARK, SAN DIEGO COUNTY

by D. L. True and C. W. Meighan

The data described herein were collected primarily during archaeological surveys conducted within the boundaries of Palomar Mountain State Park. These surveys were supported in part by the State of California Department of Parks and Recreation. This support and the generous assistance of park personnel in residence at the time is gratefully acknowledged.

Although the area included within the state park boundaries probably does not include territory belonging to the village of Molpa, it does represent an excellent example of the upland summer camp situation described in the text. Most of the park area is included in the summer camp territory of the Pauma village. Because of the proximity of the two village groups (Pauma and Cuca/Molpa) and the nearly identical characteristics of the village sites and the terrain, data from the Pauma summer camps are seen as relevant to the understanding of the Molpa settlement pattern and subsistence, and to the definition of the San Luis Rey II life-way in general.

Most of the surveying was done in the spring of 1959. Following these initial survey efforts, several additional trips were made into the area for supplementary data, and the following year test excavations were made at site SDi-593 located adjacent to the Cedar Grove camping area within the state park. Data recovered from these test excavations are included below as appendix B.

Since the state park itself represented a small portion of the total Palomar Mountain area it was decided to include some adjacent areas in order to place the sites found in the park in broader geographic relationship. The area surveyed included the territory identified ethnographically as belonging to the village of Cuca, and thus includes as well the summer camps of the village of Molpa. All habitable areas within the park were examined for archaeological remains and sur- face collections were made when artifacts were present. Outside of the park limits collections were minimal. After the basic surveys had been completed, Luiseño in- formants were taken into the area to identify specific sites, to supply Luiseño place names, and to get general information on the subsistence and settlement patterns.

THE AREA

Palomar Mountain terminates the southwesternmost end of the Agua Tibia Mountain range, which forms part of the California Peninsular Range Province in northern San Diego County, California. The western "block" of this mountain system can be described as a series of sloping erosion surfaces occurring at increasing ele- vations from west to east culminating in the higher elevations of the Agua Tibia and Laguna mountains (see map 1 in text). The surfaces are broken by many fault and erosion-controlled irregularities, and the entire area is dissected by numerous intermittent stream chan- nels as well as a few perennial streams draining the better watered regions.

Much of the included area is classed as semi-arid and receives less than 15 inches of precipitation an- nually. This precipitation varies greatly, however, and in the higher mountains twice or three times that amount per year would not be unusual. The forty-year average for the western crest of Palomar Mountain ex- ceeds 40 inches per year. This range of precipitation is reflected in the vegetative cover as are land form variations and subsequent air drainage patterns, which create frost-free thermal belts along the lower slopes of the mountain. A dense gallery forest lined the major stream channels in prehistoric times, and large portions of the foothill area supported substantial oak groves as well as typical chaparral. The higher elevations of the mountain proper are within a transition zone and are characterized by mixed conifer and deciduous forest cover.

Palomar Mountain State Park occupies 1,724 acres of heavily wooded slopes and open mountain meadowland within this transition zone. Most of the park lies along the western and southern crest of Palomar Mountain. Terrain within the park varies from open flat-bottomed meadows to steep canyon slopes covered with nearly impenetrable thickets. Tall stands of virgin timber (Douglas fir, incense cedar, and big-coned spruce) alternate with oak groves (Quercus kellogii, Quercus chrysolepis, and some Quercus dumosa), which are scattered along the ridges and around the margins of the meadows. Even at the present time this area supports a wide variety of plant and animal life. The significance of this relatively rich environmental setting and the series of microclimatic zones which extend upward from the base of the mountain in prehistoric times, becomes more apparent when it is related to the migration and gathering patterns of the aboriginal inhabitants of the area.

Historically the Palomar Mountain region was occupied by the Luiseño (Sparkman 1908: 188-190), who represent the westernmost extension of the Shoshonean subfamily of the Uto-Aztecean linguistic stock. More specifically the area within the state park was part of the acorn-gathering territory of the Pauma village. The Pauma village was located on the south side of Pauma Creek at the western and southern base of Palomar Mountain. This is probably the same place Kroeber calls Taghanashpa, although this is not certain and present-day informants do not use this name. (Spelling of Luiseño place names here follows Kroeber, Sparkman, and White and may not be consistent with present-day linguistic usage.)

Each of the Luiseño villages in this area operated as a separate and nearly autonomous socio-economic unit and had well-defined territories, which were defended against trespass. Each village territory was distributed vertically up the mountain so that in addition to valley land around the main winter village, all had access to a strip of land on the flank of the mountain, and an area on top at an elevation near 5,000 feet. All aspects of this territory were exploited in a

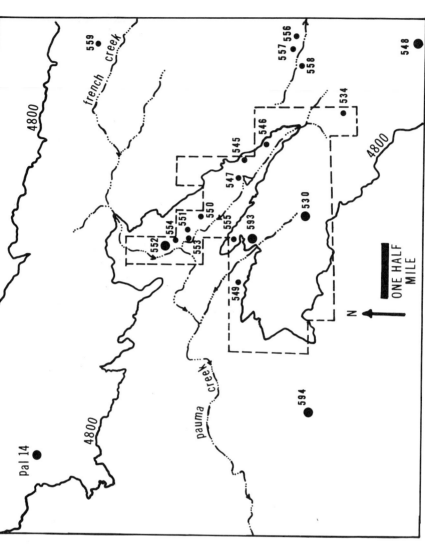

Appendix map 1. Indicates boundaries of Palomar Mountain State Park and sites in that area located during the 1958 surveys.

highly developed seasonal round extending from the valley lowlands to the mountain top. In addition, trips to the coast were made following the San Luis Rey River channel, which is described as a neutral route through the territories of other villages along the way (Raymond White 1954, personal communication). The vertical distribution of village territories had the effect of providing food resources over a long season. Within this round plant foods were collected from named locations belonging to the village as a whole (<u>tch' o (n) tcho' mi</u>) and from more specific locations belonging to a lineage or family group of some kind (<u>tch' o onum</u>). The main route connecting the Pauma winter village and the Palomar summer camps belonging to it is indicated on map 4 in the text. This trail was known as <u>pum-a-lum-pomi-la-lach</u>. The Pauma village territory on the mountain top was known collectively as Wavamai and includes most of the territory contained in the present state park as well as some possible land on Morgan Hill to the northwest (see map 1 in the appendix and map 2 in the text).

THE SITES

Thirty-one sites were located for the mountain top as a whole. This figure probably does not represent more than 25 percent of the actual number of sites to be found in this area. It does include the majority of the important villages in the western sector, and within the park proper it probably includes most of the sites of all sizes. Most of the eastern portion of the mountain was not surveyed because it was private property at the time and permission to enter could not be obtained. In general sites are located on ridges, knolls or exposed slopes along water courses, or marginal to open meadowlands. All were in some proximity to oak groves. Several of these locations were seasonally utilized as recently as World War I, and occasionally gathering trips were still made by some of the older Indians as recently as 1949.

No ceremonial sites were recorded and no pictograph locations could be found on the mountain. References in the literature (Steward 1929: 90) to pictographs

supposedly located on Palomar Mountain undoubtedly refe
to sites found on the lower slopes near the winter villages (see also True 1954: 68-72). A substantial amoun
of survey time was expended looking for surviving rem-
nants of bark structures described by Sparkman as typical summer houses for this area (Sparkman 1908: 212-213
None of these structures was located within the park
boundaries, but two were found on sites in the adjacent
territory. The first was located at the site designate
SDi-548 (Palomar 19). This appears to have been the
summer camp area for the village of Cuca. It was named
by one informant as the place Chat-po-pusa. It is not
altogether certain that this is the name of the site
proper, or simply refers to the larger area within whic
the site is located. Often both names are the same
(see appendix map 1, and map 4 in the text). The secon
structure was located at the site designated SDi-535.
This location is known as Jaculi and is described as a
summer camp place for the people from La Jolla or
Japicha (see map 4 in the text). In both cases the
structures were on private property, and permission to
make a detailed investigation could not be obtained. A
similar feature described by Wood (1937: 24) as a
sweat house could not be located, and it is presumed
that it has been destroyed.

The mountain sites included in this survey can be
divided into two general categories:

1. Camping locations for individual lineages or
   family groups marked by a well-developed midden deposit, a substantial number of bedrock
   mortars, and other indications of occupancy
   over some extended period of time (summer
   villages).

2. Samll temporary camps or gathering stations
   marked by one or two bedrock mortars usually
   small and poorly developed), a bare trace of
   midden, and only an occasional artifact
   (temporary camps).

Summer Villages of the Pauma People

The sites described below represent summer village locations for important family groups from the village of Pauma. All are located within the territory designated by Luiseño informants as Wavamai.

SDi-530

This site is located in the area presently designated as the Silver Crest picnic area within the state park (see appendix map 1). The area was designated Pa-ku-ka by Luiseño informants, but it was not possible to determine if this was the specific name of the village, or the area within which the village was located. Most of the site has been covered with decomposed granite as part of the picnic-ground development, but a well-developed midden is exposed at several points around the margins of this covered area. Erosion cuts along the western margin indicate a midden depth of some 36 inches. The midden itself is a dark ashy deposit containing charcoal, chipping waste, and occasional artifacts. The central feature of the site is a concentration of bedrock mortars. A total of 136 mortars was recorded, and it is certain that more are covered by outwash and heavy deposits of leaf mold. The mortars range in size from 3 to 14 inches in diameter and up to 14 inches deep. In addition to these deep round-bottomed elements, 10 milling areas (bedrock metates) were noted.

Several of the boulder outcroppings here also include small pit-like depressions suggesting miniature or incipient mortars. These range in size from 1 to 2 inches in diameter and up to 3/4 inches deep. Some are located on horizontal surfaces and could have been used for some kind of processing activity. Others, however, are found on nearly vertical surfaces, and it is difficult to see how they could have served for grinding or pounding activities. These elements tend to occur in clusters and in some instances are heavily covered with lichen, suggesting relatively greater age than the adjacent bedrock mortars. No function is suggested by informants but it is possible that these pits are manifestations of pit and groove petroglyphs described for several other parts of California (Heizer and Baumhoff 1962: 234-238).

Although this was obviously an important site and was extensively used for a long period of time, relatively few artifacts have been recovered. The dearth of surface artifacts is not surprising, however, when the historical circumstances of the location are considered. For the past several years this has been a state park picnic area, and literally thousands of people walk over the site during any given summer. It has been a favorite lookout point for decades and near the turn of the century it was the location of a resort hotel. The few artifacts recovered here are listed in appendix table 5. (Artifact types used in this appendix follow those used in the text. Sites are listed by SDi numbers when possible, otherwise local designations are given.)

SDi-593

The site here is located at the present Cedar Grove campground within the state park. The area is known to Pauma informants as Pee-nav-angña, but, as with the other locations so far described, it was not possible to pinpoint this as the specific name of the site itself. It seems likely that it is, however.

The midden here starts along the upper part of a low knoll (Cedar Grove) and extends downslope some 50 to 60 yards into a small meadow and watercourse, which represents part of the headwaters of Pauma Creek. This slope has a southern exposure and is favorably situated for camping well into the fall season. The site covers some two acres of ground. Part of the midden deposit has been disturbed by campsite construction. Scattered apple trees along the eastern edge of the site are evidence of some earlier attempt to farm the area, so it is likely that the surface has been disturbed at various times in the past. Part of the site is covered by a dense thicket of chokecherry (Prunus demissa), a plant described as an important Luiseño subsistence item. The midden is dark and ashy and typical of late sites in the area. Scattered bedrock mortars are found at several

locations on the site. Some bedrock milling surfaces
(bedrock metates) are also present. Artifacts recovered
from the survey and from a preliminary excavation of the
site the following year are described in appendix B
below.

SDi-552

This site is a smaller village or camping area located near the junction of lower Doane Creek and French
Creek. At this point the two tributaries combine to form
Pauma Creek. The midden area here appears to cover
about 1/2 acre. A conspicuous bedrock outcropping overlooking French Creek contains several bedrock mortars
and milling stones (metates). The area has been gleaned
by hikers for many years, and surface artifacts are
scarce. It appears that the deposit itself has not been
disturbed. This location was designated Pos-ik-na by
Luiseño informants. Artifacts recovered during the
surveys are included in appendix table 5.

Palomar 14

Palomar 14 is located on Morgan Hill northwest of
Palomar state park (see appendix map 1). At the time
of the survey, informants reported that this site belonged to the Pauma village. This would make it part of
the territory called Wavamai. However, this is actually
in the area called Sch-o and Sparkman (1908: 192) described "Shoau" as the place "the Pala Indians had their
encampment during the acorn gathering season". The location of the site tends to support Sparkman, and it is
more likely that it was part of the territory utilized
by people from Agua Tibia or Pala, rather than by people from Pauma. This was probably the case in earlier
prehistoric times, although as part of a more recent agglutination of local territories it may well have fallen
into the Pauma sphere of influence. In any case, there
is evidence that it is very close to the Pauma/Pala
boundary, and the locale has been used in recent times
by Pauma people as grazing area for livestock.

Because no other resources from the Pala area are
included in this report, and because of the possible

confusion of its affiliation, this site is included here as an element in the Pauma settlement.

The site itself is situated west of the high point of Morgan Hill at an elevation of 5,400 feet. The area is characterized by an oak parkland and mixed coniferous forest. A small flat adjacent to a large boulder outcropping contains a well-developed midden. No testing was attempted during this visit, but it was obvious that this was an area of some importance. The midden was dark and ashy, included substantial amounts of chipping waste, and artifacts were quite common. This is clearly an important San Luis Rey II site. This area is known to informants as La-kal-ka. However, the name may refer to the locality, to the site, or to a rocky cliff adjacent to the site which is important in the local folklore.

SDi-594

This important summer camp is also outside the state park boundaries. It is, however, within the territory designated Wavamai and was used by the people from Pauma. This is an extensive site (or series of sites) and is scattered over nearly ten acres in the vicinity of Nathan Harrison Spring. At least two distinct midden areas can be detected here along with scattered bedrock outcroppings containing mortars and milling stones (bedrock metates). Local informants describe this as an acorn gathering location and a place to get gooseberries in season. Because this site was outside the park boundaries and the cooperation of the owner was somewhat qualified, no great amount of time was spent investigating the resources here. A casual examination of the surface was made on one trip, and a single test pit was dug on a second visit to check the depth of the deposit. Artifacts and culturally modified soil extended to a depth of 36 inches. Artifacts taken from this test pit as well as the few items collected from the surface are included in appendix table 5. Appendix table 6 indicates the provenience of the test pit artifacts by depth.

The locality is known as To-ko-ma. This almost certainly refers to the same place Sparkman calls

Tok-a-mai (1908: 192).

Temporary Camps and Gathering Stations in the Pauma Territory (Wavamai)

In addition to the important villages described above, several other sites were located within the bounds of the Pauma village summer camping area. These probably represent seed-collecting stations, and most likely are contemporary with the main camps described above. However, in some cases at least it is possible that these are manifestations of an earlier San Luis Rey I occupancy of this area.

Site SDi-549 is located in the meadow adjacent to Doane Pond and the county camp area. Luiseño informants called this place Pas-mai. This may be a designation for a fairly important summer camp site, or it may be that the informants were saying Pais-vi and there was some misunderstanding with regard to its exact provenience. Pais-vi is the term generally given to Iron Springs which is nearby, but in another drainage (see Sparkman 1908: 192).

At the present time evidence of prehistoric occupancy here is limited. It is an area where considerable construction work and surface modification has taken place, and it is possible that more extensive evidence was destroyed in the construction of the county camp facility, Doane Pond, and the adjacent parking lot. In any case, the present investigation recovered only scattered and minimal evidence of use.

Sites SDi-554, 553, 551 and 550 are scattered along the margins of lower Doane Valley. All appear to be temporary collecting stations with minimal evidence of use, limited to an occasional small bedrock mortar or bedrock milling area. In some cases there is evidence of slight soil discoloration but artifacts are rare. Pauma informants did not name any of these locations.

Similarly in upper Doane Valley there are three small stations. Two of these were given site designations (SDi-545, 546). Another site on upper Chimney Creek (SDi-534) may also belong with the upper Doane Complex. SDi-555 is an acorn-processing station

probably belonging to the village at Cedar Grove
SDi-593). Evidence of occupancy here is limited to bedrock mortars. No attempt was made to glean artifacts
from any of the above described sites. When noted,
however, they were picked up and are included in appendi.
table 5.

Summer Villages on Palomar
Outside of the Pauma Territory

Because the present investigations were directed
toward the resources of the state park, information on
sites outside the park is less detailed. Surveys were
mostly limited to examination of the more important
sites. The majority of these are known to surviving
Luiseño and nearly all have names. No excavations were
made and only casual collection of surface artifacts was
attempted. All sites in this grouping are on private
land and most owners preferred a minimal level of investigation. In several areas, in fact, it was impossible to get permission to survey, and it is almost
certain that at least two additional important villages
and numerous small stations are not included in this
resume. Future work in portions of upper French Valley,
Mendenhall Valley, and Barker Valley is vital to the
completion of this survey.

Data available at the present time on sites outside
of the Pauma Territory is presented below in appendix
tables 1, 2, 3, and 4.

APPENDIX TABLE 1

Summer Camps or Villages in the Cuca/Molpa Territory

Site SDi-548

Location: Southwestern rim of Palomar Mountain at an elevation of 5300 feet (see appendix map 1).

Affiliation: San Luis Rey II. Probably key summer camp for Cuca Village. Informants indicate area known by name of Chat-po-pusa.

Comment: Bedrock mortars, developed midden, remains of cedar bark structure (see appendix table 5).

Site SDi-540

Location: Marginal to Iron Springs Creek approximately 1/4 mile southwest of Sunday School flats (see map 4 in text). The elevation here is 5,000 feet.

Affiliation: San Luis Rey II. Important summer camp for village of Cuca or Molpa. Specific name for site uncertain, but probably village or Mok-wan-mai. Sparkman (1908: 192) lists Mok-wan-mai as "an old village on Palomar". Recent informants indicated this general area as the location of Mok-wan-mai but did not specifically identify the actual village site itself.

Comment: Bedrock mortars, developed midden, numerous artifacts. Clearly an important site. The area was utilized for acorn-collecting purposes at least as recently as 1950.

SDi-1286

Location: Vicinity of Crestline camp area. Palomar Mountain elevation about 5,400 feet (see map 4 in text).

Affiliation: San Luis Rey II. Camp area and acorn-
gathering location for Cuca or Molpa
Village. The locality is known as Pav-la
Sparkman (1908: 192) described Pav-la as
the "place where the Kuca or Potrero en-
camped while gathering acorns on Palomar"

Comment: Only scattered evidence of occupancy was
located in the present survey. No major
site or developed midden could be found.
However, there has been extensive construction in part of the area. This plus
heavy ground cover in some places and
several private cabin areas with restricted entry limited the survey and may account for the failure to locate the site
that should be here. Scattered artifacts
and a few bedrock mortars can be found
in this area.

APPENDIX TABLE 2

Summer Camps or Villages in the
Japicha-La Jolla Territory

Site SDi-535

Location: Low knoll on headwaters of Cedar Creek at
elevation of 4,900 feet (see map 4 in
text).

Affiliation: San Luis Rey II summer camp area. Almost
certainly belonged to people from Japicha.
(Japicha previously was a community similar to Cuca and La Jolla with its own
territory, winter village, and summer camp
areas on the mountain. In historic times
it has ceased to function as an autonomous entity and is now considered by most
people to be part of La Jolla.) The site
here is known as Cha-culi.

(134)

(Sparkman 1908: 192) lists Cha-culi as "an old village site on Palomar".

Comment: This is probably the most impressive site examined so far in this survey. It includes numerous bedrock mortars, bedrock mortars superimposed over bedrock milling areas (metates), pairs of bedrock mortars and mortars in combination with oval-basined metates. The midden is dark and ashy and includes large amounts of refuse, chipping waste and numerous artifacts. Remains of a cedar bark structure were standing at the time of the surveys. Cha-culi has been identified as the ancestral acorn gathering place of the Cueva family (Mrs. A. McCormick 1953, personal communication).

Site SDi-539

Location: Southwestern rim of Palomar Mountain at an elevation of 4,600 feet. The site overlooks the San Luis Rey River Canyon some 2,000 feet below (see map 4 in text).

Affiliation: San Luis Rey II. A summer camp site for people from Japicha or La Jolla. This is the location of the village called Shau-tush-ma. Sparkman (1908: 192) does not locate Shau-tush-ma but he lists it as the place where the "Yap-icha Indians had their encamp-ment during the acorn gathering season on Palomar". The name was confirmed by informants during the present survey.

Comment: The site here is connected with winter villages in the La Jolla area by a trail complex that can still be identified (see map 4 in text). No artifact collections were made from SDi-539. Artifacts and features there are typically San Luis Rey II.

Site SDi-537

Location: A point of land at an elevation of 4,400 feet overlooking the San Luis Rey River canyon (see map 4 in text).

Affiliation: San Luis Rey II. No ethnographic description or designation was obtained for this locality. It appears to have been an important summer camp, however, and is connected by well-developed trails with the village locations in the San Luis Rey River canyon below (see map 4 in text). This is almost certainly a summer camp location for the La Jolla people.

Comment: The site contains a well-developed midden, numerous bedrock mortars, chipping waste, and potsherds. A few artifacts were collected from the surface here (see appendix table 5).

Site SDi-536

Location: Eastern edge of Dyche Valley at an elevation of 4,400 feet (see map 4 in text).

Affiliation: San Luis Rey II. This place is described as a summer camp location for the La Jolla people. It is given the name Malava by Luiseño informants. Sparkman (1908: 192) describes Malava as "an old village site on Palomar".

Comment: No collections were made from this site. It has a typical San Luis Rey II assemblage, a well-developed midden and several bedrock mortars.

Site SDi-538

Location: Southeastern end of Will Valley at an
                 elevation of 4,000 feet (see map 4 in
                 text).

Affiliation: Location, general midden characteristics,
                 and artifacts suggest that this is a San
                 Luis Rey II site. It was almost certainly
                 a summer camp area for people from La
                 Jolla. However, no ethnographic con-
                 firmation of this was possible.

Comment: This site has been badly damaged by road
                 construction. A few artifacts were col-
                 lected from the road-cut surfaces (see
                 appendix table 5).

APPENDIX TABLE 3

Short Term Camps and Stations in the
Cuca-Molpa Territory

Site SDi-558

Location: South side of Iron Springs Creek just west
                 of Sunday School flats (see appendix map 1).

Affiliation: Unknown but probably San Luis Rey II.
                 Iron Springs is cited as the place of
                 origin for the red pigment used for paint
                 by the Luiseño (Harrington 1933: 141-144;
                 Max Peters 1957, personal communication).

Comment: This is a small area with minimal indi-
                 cation of use. There was scant alteration
                 of the soil and no diagnostic artifacts.
                 At least one small bedrock mortar was
                 present in the immediate area.

(137)

Site SDi-557

Location: North side of Iron Spring Creek across from SDi-558 (see appendix map 1).

Affiliation: Same as indicated for SDi-558 above.

Comment: Minimal indication of use. No diagnosti artifacts.

Site SDi-556

Location: North side of Iron Creek, just north of Sunday School flat (see appendix map 1).

Affiliation: Same as SDi-558 above.

Comment: Minimal indication of use. No way to kno which group used these stations. Because the red paint pigments were important in all of the communities, it is possible that this area was some kind of common area shared by more than one group. Geographically it appears to be close to the boundary separating the Pauma and Cuca territory.

---

(138)

APPENDIX TABLE 4

Short Term Camps and Stations
Outside of the Cuca/Molpa Area

Site Palomar 13

Location: Eastern margin of Palomar mass on the site of the present Palomar Mountain school.

Affiliation: Unknown. Appears to be a nonpottery location. Ownership of this territory uncertain. Site is probably not San Luis Rey II.

Comment: Minimal evidence of soil alteration. Occasional artifacts found on surface and during construction of school building. No features were noted. This part of Palomar Mountain was not systematically surveyed because of restricted entry.

Site SDi-559

Location: North side of upper French Valley (see appendix map 1).

Affiliation: Uncertain. Could be part of Pauma territory but boundaries in this area are not clear.

Comment: Minimal evidence of occupancy. Some soil alteration. Artifacts not common. This is a possible San Luis Rey II camp, but it is impossible to state for sure because no diagnostic artifacts were reported.

APPENDIX TABLE 5

Artifact Distributions, Palomar Mountain Sites

	SDi-530	SDi-593	SDi-552	SDi-549	SDi-547	SDi-554	SDi-553	SDi-551	SDi-550	SDi-558	SDi-555	SDi-534	SDi-535	SDi-536	SDi-537	SDi-538	SDi-539	SDi-540	Pal-14	SDi-548	SDi-559
Projectile Points																					
Type 1	1		3							1		1							2		
Type 2	2		1																		
Type 3																1		1			
Type 3-S			1																		
Type 2-S	1		1																		
Nondiagnostic	4									4					3	1			1		
Manos	1		5		1						1									1	1
Beads																					

(140)

APPENDIX TABLE 5 (continued)

	SDi-530	SDi-593	SDi-552	SDi-549	SDi-547	SDi-554	SDi-553	SDi-551	SDi-550	SDi-558	SDi-555	SDi-534	SDi-535	SDi-536	SDi-537	SDi-538	SDi-539	SDi-540	Pal-14	SDi-548	SDi-559
Shell Ornaments			1																		
Knives																					
Conventional	1		1								2					1					
Nondiagnostic	1																				
Irregular flake	1		1															1			
Used flake	1		2									1									
Drills			2																		
Scrapers																					
Small domed	1		1																		
Heavy flake	1																				

(141)

APPENDIX TABLE 5 (continued)

	SDi-559	SDi-548	Pal-14	SDi-540	SDi-539	SDi-538	SDi-537	SDi-536	SDi-535	SDi-534	SDi-555	SDi-558	SDi-550	SDi-551	SDi-553	SDi-554	SDi-547	SDi-549	SDi-552	SDi-593	SDi-530
Small flake																					
Worked Flakes				2															4		
Cores																					2
Worked Sherds																					1
Tizon Sherds		41	30	87		16	5				27		1	1					76		17
Sherds		1	1	1																	
Bone Artifacts																			4		
Historic																					1
Artifacts		2	1																		

(142)

APPENDIX TABLE 6

Artifact Distribution Site SDi-594 (Test Pit 1)

	Surface	0"–6"	6"–12"	12"–18"	18"–24"	24"–30"	30"–36"	Totals
Projectile Points								
Type 1	2			2				4
Type 2					1			1
Type 2S	1							1
Type 3S	1							1
Manos	2			1	1		1	5
Shell Ornaments		1						1
Knives								
Conventional	1							1
Irregular Flake	2							2
Heavy Flake								
Drills	1					1		2
Scrapers								
Small Domed	1							1

(143)

APPENDIX TABLE 6 (continued)

	Surface	0"-6"	6"-12"	12"-18"	18"-24"	24"-30"	30"-36"	Totals
Worked Flakes	2	1		1				4
Tizon Sherds	34	17	6	9	7	3		76
Bone Artifacts								
Awls	1	1		1	1			4
Totals	48	20	6	14	10	4	1	
Serrated								

APPENDIX TABLE 7

PARTIAL INVENTORY OF ARTIFACTS FROM SDi-535

Projectile Points	
Type 1	22
Type 2	6
Type 3	2
Type 4	1
Type 5	2
Potsherds	
Tizon Brown	149
Intrusive	
Colorado River Wares	8

See acknowledgements in text relating to site.

APPENDIX B. ARTIFACTS FROM SDi-593
PALOMAR MOUNTAIN STATE PARK, CALIFORNIA

by
Smiley Karst

Excavations at SDi-593 were carried out in 1961 by a field class from the University of California, Los Angeles, under the direction of C. N. Warren. Seven test pits were excavated and features associated with the site were mapped (see appendix A for the location of SDi-593 and general data on the area). The midden at SDi-593 ranges in depth from a few inches near the margins of the site to about 42 inches in the deepest areas. Pottery was recovered to a depth of 24 inches. This suggests a multiple component site with San Luis Rey II material overlying a San Luis Rey I component. Except for the ceramics, however, the midden appeared to lack stratification. There was some indication of soil color change below the 35-inch level and much of the 36 to 42-inch level was sterile. The deposit itself is a fine textured sandy loam that seems to be mostly outwash deposition from an adjacent knoll. This basic soil has been modified through time as a result of the occupancy of the site. It now includes substantial amounts of charcoal, humus, and other indications of other organic materials generally associated with late sites in this region.

The excavated sample was dug in 6-inch levels and all material was passed through a 1/4-inch mesh screen. The seven excavated units, plus a surface-collected sample made during the original park surveys, yielded 306 artifacts. Suggested types and artifact frequencies may be seen in appendix tables 8 and 9. Appendix table 10 adjusts these types to those used in the text to facilitate comparisons. Some additional comment on the recovered specimens follows:

GRINDING IMPLEMENTS

Three rock outcroppings on the site proper contained bedrock mortars. These were similar to mortars found on other late sites in the area and duplicate those reported from the site at Molpa.

Seventeen whole or partial manos were recovered. Three of these were bifacial, eight unifacial, the remainder being nondiagnostic for this attribute. The majority (15) were made of granitic rock of one kind or another. One was identified as basalt and another sandstone.

Two artifacts were identified as pestles. One, made of schist, has a nearly rectangular shape and has been worked on all four sides. The second is only slightly modified and is quite heavy. This is a typical pestle for the San Luis Rey II complex, and similar artifacts are commonly recovered in this area (see pl. 9 f for a similar artifact that is typical in size, form and degree of modification). The specimen from SDi-593 is 30 cm. long, 18 cm. wide, and 6 cm. thick.

No metates were recovered from this site although this seems to be a relatively common implement on other sites in the area.

PROJECTILE POINTS

Sixty-three partial or complete projectile points were recovered from this site (see appendix B fig. 1.) Forty-three of these were complete enough to be classified as to type. Thirty-three (76.7 percent) are triangular with concave, covex, or straight bases and are typical of most points found in this area in other contexts (McCown, 1948; McCown, 1955; Meighan, 1954, True, 1966; True, Meighan, and Crew, this volume). The length of these points varies from 1.5 to 3.5 centimeters with an average of 2.3 centimeters. The width varies from 1.0 to 2.5, averaging 1.5 centimeters. My Types 1, 2, 3, and 4 represent this group. My Type 5 which is side notched with an indented base typically makes up but a small part of the points found in collections from this part of southern California. Three examples

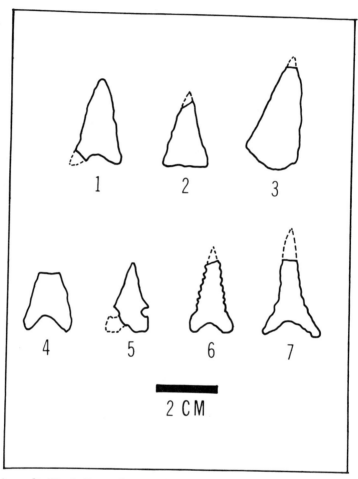

Appendix Fig. 1. Projectile point forms from the excavations at SDi–593.

of this type were found at SDi-593, averaging 2.1 cm. in length and 1.3 cm. in width. Only one example of my Type 6 was found. Precise serrations along the upper edges of the point and incipient side notching near the base distinguish Type 6 from Type 5. The single type point is 2.5 cm. long and 1.5 cm. wide. My Type 6y is represented by six specimens. This form is different from those described above in that it is narrow relative to its width along most of its length and flares outwardly sharply at 140 degrees, forming a deeply indented fishtail base. Three of these forms are serrated. Forms similar to this from other collections in this area sometimes have rounded cross sections near the tip and some indication that they may have been used as a drill. Type 7 points average 1.7 cm. in width. No whole specimens are included in the present sample.

The projectile points from SDi-593 average 2.3 centimeters in length. Quartz is the material most frequently used in the manufacture of these points. Of the forty-three identifiable specimens 79 percent are made of quartz. Three artifacts are made of black obsidian, two are basaltic, two a local chert, and one is an unidentified beige-colored stone.

BEADS

Two beads were found at this site. One was a shell disc made from a side section of an *Olivella*. The other was a blue glass trade bead.

POTTERY

Two hundred and twenty sherds were found at SDi-593, all but two of them on the surface or within the two upper levels of the excavation. The pottery here is the type designed Palomar Brown (Meighan 1959; Euler 1959). The few rim sherds present have both direct and recurved forms.

MISCELLANEOUS

A small incised slab was recovered from the second level of Unit 7 (6-21 inches). At the time of recovery it was fragmented and has been partially restored. This item is illustrated in plate 13.

A curved stem fragment of pottery pipe was recovered in the fifth level of Unit 4. This fragment was 7.0 cm. long and originally had a flanged handle. It resembles one depicted by Iovin (1963: 108) and is a form typically found in the Diegueño territory to the south. Diegueño bow pipes are not uncommon, however, in both the Diegueño and Luiseño territories (McCown 1948, 1955).

DISCUSSION

Almost all of the artifact forms described above are found in collections from one or another of several nearby sites of known late date.

At the Fallbrook site, McCown found 29 projectile points. These include my Types 1, 2, 4, and 5, and possibly 3. He also reports granite cobble pestles, bifacial and unifacial manos, scrapers, hammerstones, a pottery pipe, and 247 vessel sherds. The sherds are described as resembling northern Diegueño ware (McCown 1948). The pottery described here is clearly Tizon Brown, and the total assemblage is representative of of the San Luis Rey II complex.

At a site in the San Vicente lake bed (in Diegueño territory) McCown recovered my point Types 1, 2, and probably 5. He does not illustrate or quantify his artifacts, however, and this comparison is based on his description of the points. He described them as being "predominately triangular in shape with the base varying from straight to a deep V-shaped indentation". Eight points are described as notched and 2 as serrated. He found a total of 64 projectile points at this site.

The San Vicente lake-bed site also produced Olivella disc beads and pottery. The pottery is described as reddish brown with black smudged spots. The described shapes resemble those found in the Luiseño territory. McCown suggests that all the artifacts in this collection are like those found in the camps of the northern Diegueño (McCown 1945).

The village at Temeku also excavated by McCown, yielded 754 partial or complete projectile points. The Vail site located nearby produced an additional 41 (McCown 1955). These include my Types 1, 2, 4, and 5. McCown also reports bedrock mortars and metates. Fifty-eight manos were recovered at Temeku. One mano was reported from the Vail site. Heavy pestles similar to the one from SDi-593 were common. He reports in addition 22 hammerstones and 73 scrapers.

Two pieces of slate incised with cross-hatching resemble the incised tablet from 593. Beads were common at Temeku. Fourteen glass beads and 15 Olivella discs beads were recovered and from Vail, 26 glass beads and 60 Olivella discs.

Fragments of curved tubular pipes were also present at Temeku. Pottery was represented by 6,726 sherds. Most of these were clearly Tizon ware made using the paddle and anvil method. A few, however, appear to have been molded by hand. Both direct and recurved rims are represented.

Meighan (1954) reports 61 points including my Types 1, 2, 3, 4, and 5 from a San Luis Rey I site located on Frey creek some ten miles southeast of Temeku. This site also produced Olivella shell beads, bedrock mortars and metates, manos (30), pestles, scrapers, and hammerstones.

The site of Molpa (described in the text) is an historic Luiseño site. Excavations there produced my point Types 1, 3, and 4. Tizon brown pottery is also found here. (See the text for additional detail on artifacts from this site.)

The winter village of the Pauma people (SDi-616) has yielded my point Types 1 and 2. Although quantification in most instances is inadequate for precise comparisons, it appears that most of the sites cited above share nearly all of the characteristic artifacts recovered from SDi-593. A comparison of these artifacts with those published by Iovin in her survey of Luiseño culture elements suggests a clear-cut similarity except for my point Types 6 and 7. Some artifacts listed by Iovin were not found at SDi-593, but the overall configuration is near enough to suggest that this site should be placed in the San Luis Rey II pattern (1963: 83-130).

Descriptive Table of Specimens, SDi-593

Artifact type	Total	Material	Average size
Manos			
bifacial	3	granite	11.0 cm. x 9.0 cm.
monfacial	8	granite, sandstone	11.0 cm. x 9.75 cm.
fragments	14	"metamorphic stone"	
		granite, basalt	
Pestles	2		
(Of the two described, one is probably a mano worked on four sides; the other seems too large and heavy to be used as a pestle.)			
Projectile points			
Type 1 concave base	13	quartz (11)	2.5 cm. length
		obsidian (1)	1.8 cm. width
		? (1)	
Type 2 triangular	4	quartz (4)	1.9 cm. length
			1.4 cm. width
Type 3 leaf-shaped	4	quartz (4)	3.3 cm. length
			1.6 cm. width

APPENDIX TABLE 8 (continued)

Artifact type	Total	Material	Average size
Type 4 "swallowtail"	12	quartz (9) ? (3)	2.2 cm. length 1.2 cm. width
Type 5 sidenotched, concave base	3	quartz (1) obsidian (2)	2.1 cm. length 1.3 cm. width
Type 6 serrated	1	? (1)	2.5 cm. length 1.5 cm. width
Type 7 "fishtail"	6	quartz (5) ? (1)	1.5 cm. maximum width
Unclassifiable	20	quartz (1) ?	
Miscellaneous Stone objects Scrapers	10	quartz ( ) ? ( )	
Hammerstones	2	basalt (1) ? (1)	7.0 cm. diam.

APPENDIX TABLE 8 (continued)

Artifact type	Total	Material	Average size
Chips and flakes	86	quartz (53) basalt (11) obsidian (3) chert (15) jasper (1) ? (3)	5.8 cm. x 5.6 cm.
Cross-hatched stone slab	1	limestone (2)	
Beads trade bead	1	blue glass	0.6 cm. diam. 0.5 cm. length
disc bead	1	Olivella	0.5 cm. diam. 0.1 cm. length
Pipe fragment	1	pottery	8.1 cm. length 3.35 cm. diam.
Worked bone cylinder	1	bone	7.3 cm. length 2.0 cm. diam.

APPENDIX TABLE 8 (continued)

Artifact type	Total	Material	Average size
Polished bone fragments	3	bone	7.7 cm. length 1.9 cm. width
Burnt mammal bone	5	bone	
Unmodified organic material (shell, bone, tooth)	95		

APPENDIX TABLE 9

Frequency of Pottery Sherds

Location	Number of Sherds	Depth
---	54	surface
Pit 5	2	0-6 inches
Pit 7	63	0-6 inches
Pit 3	3	6-12 inches
Pit 5	22	6-12 inches
Pit 7	49	6-12 inches
Pit 3	2	18-24 inches

APPENDIX TABLE 10

Projectile Point Type Comparisons

SDi-593 and Molpa Report

Molpa	SDi-593
Type 1	Type 1 Type 4 Type 7
Type I serrated	Type 6
Type 2	Type 2
Type 3	Type 3
Type 5	Type 5

BIBLIOGRAPHY

Baumhoff, M., and J. S. Byrne
1959. Desert Side Notched Points as a Time Marker in California. University of California Archaeological Survey Report 48: 32-65. Berkeley.

Beardsley, Richard K., et al.
1956. Functional and Evolutionary Implications of Community Patterning. In Seminars in Archaeology: 1955. Memoir No. 11, Society for American Archaeology, vol. 22, no. 2, part 2. Salt Lake City.

Binford, L. R.
1964. A Consideration of Archaeological Research Design. American Antiquity, vol. 29, no. 4, pp. 425-441.
1968. Post Pleistocene Adaptations. In New Perspectives in Archaeology, edited by S. R. Binford and L. R. Binford. Pp. 313-341. Chicago: Aldine Publishing Co.

Burnett, E. K.
1944. Inlaid Stone and Bone Artifacts from Southern California. Contributions from the Museum of the American Indian Heye Foundation, vol. 13. New York.

Colton, Harold S., editor
1958. Pottery Types of the Southwest. Museum of Northern Arizona Ceramic Series, no. 30. Flagstaff.

Davis, Edward H.
1919. The Diegueño Ceremony of the Death Images. Museum of the American Indian, Heye Foundation, vol. 5, no. 2. New York.

Du Bois, Constance Goddard
1905. Religious Ceremonies and Myths of the Mission Indians. American Anthropologist, n. s., 7: 620-629. Lancaster.
1908. The Religion of the Luiseño Indians. University of California Publications in American Archaeology and Ethnology, 8: 69-173. Berkeley.

Eberhart, Hal
  n.d.   Report on an Archaeological Survey Near Rincon
         Indian Reservation San Diego County, California.
         (Ms. on file with Department of Anthropology,
         University of California, Los Angeles, 1952.)
Ellis, A. J., and C. H. Lee
  1919. Geology and Ground Waters of Western Part of
         San Diego County. U. S. Geological Survey
         Water Supply Paper 446: 1-321. Washington.
Euler, Robert
  1959. Comparative Comments on California Pottery.
         University of California Archaeological Survey,
         Annual Report, 1958-59. Los Angeles.
Euler, Robert, and Henry R. Dobyns
  1958. Tizon Brownware, a Descriptive Revision. In
         Pottery Types of the Southwest. Edited by
         Harold S. Colton. Museum of Northern Arizona
         Ceramic Series, no. 3 D. Flagstaff.
Harner, Michael J.
  1958. Lowland Patayan Phases in the Lower Colorado
         River Valley and Colorado Desert. University
         of California Archaeological Survey Reports
         42: 93-97. Berkeley.
Harrington, J. P.
  1933. Annotations in Chinigchinich. Edited by P. T.
         Hanna. Santa Ana, California: Fine Arts Press.
  1934. A New Original Version of Boscanas Historical
         Accounts of the San Juan Capistrano Indians of
         Southern California. Smithsonian Miscellaneous
         Collections, vol. 92, no. 4. Washington, D.C.
Heizer, Robert F., and Martin A. Baumhoff
  1962. Prehistoric Rock Art of Nevada and Eastern
         California. Berkeley and Los Angeles: Univer-
         sity of California Press.
Iovin, June
  1963. A Summary Description of Luiseño Material Cul-
         ture. University of California Archaeological
         Survey Annual Report, 1962-63. Pp. 79-130.
         Los Angeles.
Jennings, Jesse J. D.
  1957. Danger Cave. Memoirs of the Society for Ameri-
         can Archaeology, no. 14. Salt Lake City.

Kroeber, Alfred L.
1925. Handbook of the Indians of California. Bureau of American Ethnology, Bull. 78. Washington.

Kowta, Makoto
1969. The Sayles Complex: A Late Milling Stone Assemblage from Cajon Pass and the Ecological Implications of its Scraper Planes. University of California Publications in Anthropology, vol. 6. Berkeley and Los Angeles.

Kushner, Gilbert
1970. A Consideration of Some Processual Designs for Archaeology as Anthropology. American Antiquity, vol. 35, no. 2, pp. 125-132. Salt Lake City.

Lanning, Edward P.
1963. Archaeology of the Rose Springs Site INY-372. University of California Publications in American Archaeology and Ethnology, 49 (3): 237-336. Berkeley.

Larsen, Esper S., Jr.
1948. Batholith and Associated Rocks of Corona, Elsinore, and San Luis Rey Quandrangles, Southern California. Geological Society of America. Memoir 29. New York.
1951. Crystalline Rocks of the Corona, Elsinore, and San Luis Rey Quadrangles, Southern California. In Crystalline Rocks of South Western California. Bulletin 159, California Division of Mines. San Francisco.

Mann, John F.
1955. Geology of a Portion of the Elsinore Fault Zone, California. Special Report 43, California Division of Mines. San Francisco.

McCown, B. E.
1945. An Archaeological Survey of San Vicente Lake Bed, San Diego County, California. American Antiquity, 10: 255-264. Menasha.
1948. Report on Excavation Site Number 7, Fallbrook Area. Typescript for Archaeological Survey Association of Southern California.
1955. Temeku. Archaeological Survey Association of Southern California, Papers, no. 3. Los Angeles.

Meighan, C. W.
  1954. A Late Complex in Southern California Prehistory.
    Southwestern Journal of Anthropology,
    10: 215-227. Albuquerque.
  1959a. Archaeological Resources of Borrego State Park.
    University of California Archaeological Survey,
    Annual Report 1958-59. Los Angeles.
  1959b. California Cultures and the Concept of an
    Archaic Stage. American Antiquity, 24 (3);
    289-305. Salt Lake City.

Riddell, Francis A.
  1960. The Archaeology of the Karlo Site (Las-7)
    California. University of California Archae-
    ological Survey Reports, no. 53. Berkeley.

Rogers, Malcom J.
  1936. Yuman Pottery Making. San Diego Museum of Man
    Papers, no. 2. San Diego.
  1945. An Outline of Yuman Prehistory. Southwestern
    Journal of Anthropology, 1 (2): 167-198.
    Albuquerque.

Schroeder, Albert H.
  1961. Archaeological Excavations at Willow Beach,
    Arizona. University of Utah Anthropological
    Papers, no. 50. Salt Lake City.

Shumway, George, Carl L. Hubbs, and James Moriarty
  1961. Scripps Estates Site, San Diego, California:
    A La Jolla Site Dated 5460 to 7370 Years Before
    the Present. Annals of the New York Academy
    of Sciences, 93: 37-132. New York.

Sparkman, Phillip Stedman
  1908. The Culture of the Luiseño Indians. University
    of California Publications in American Archae-
    ology and Ethnology, 8: 188-234. Berkeley.

Steward, J. H.
  1929. Petroglyphs of California and Adjoining States.
    University of California Publications in Ameri-
    can Archaeology and Ethnology, vol. 26.
    Berkeley.

Strong, William Duncan
  1929. Aboriginal Society in Southern California.
    University of California Publications in Ameri-
    can Archaeology and Ethnology, vol. 26.
    Berkeley.

Thomas, David Hurst, Jr.
1971. Prehistoric Subsistence-Settlement Patterns of
       the Reese River Valley, Central Nevada. Un-
       published dissertation, Department of Anthro-
       pology, University of California, Davis.
Treganza, A. E.
1942. An Archaeological Reconnaissance of Northeastern
       Baja California and Southeastern california.
       American Antiquity, 8: 152-163.
True, D. L.
1954. Pictographs of the San Luis Rey Basin San Diego
       County, California. American Antiquity,
       20 (I): 68-72. Salt Lake City.
1957. Fired Clay Figurines from San Diego County,
       California. American Antiquity, 22:291-296.
       Salt Lake City.
1958. An Early Complex in San Diego County, California.
       American Antiquity, 23 (3): 255-263. Salt Lake
       City.
1966. Archaeological Differentiation of Shoshonean
       and Yuman Speaking Groups in Southern California.
       Unpublished Ph.D. dissertation, University of
       California, Los Angeles.
1970. Archaeological Investigations at Cuyamaca Rancho
       State Park. University of California Archae-
       ological Survey. Monograph No. 1. Los Angeles.
Warren, C. N.
1964. Culture Change and Continuity of the San Diego
       Coast. Unpublished Ph.D. dissertation, Uni-
       versity of California, Los Angeles.
Warren, C. N., and D. L. True
1961. The San Dieguito Complex and its Place in Cali-
       fornia Prehistory. University of California
       Archaeological Survey, Annual Report 1960-61.
       Los Angeles.
Warren, C. N., D. L. True, and Ardith Eudey
1961. Early Gathering Complexes of Western San Diego
       County, California. University of California
       Archaeology Survey, Annual Report, 1960-61.
       Los Angeles.

White, Raymond H.
  1963. Luiseño Social Organization. University of
        California Publications in American Archae-
        ology and Ethnology, 48 (2): 91-194.
Willey, Gordon R., and Phillip Phillips
  1958. Method and Theory in American Archaeology.
        University of Chicago Press.
Wood, Catherine M.
  1937. Palomar: From Teepee to Telescope. San Diego:
        Fry and Smith Ltd.

PLATES

PLATE 1

General view of Molpa and adjacent terrain.

PLATE 2

Features within Molpa. Arrow indicates location of Trench J.

PLATE 3
Surface features within Molpa.

PLATE 4

Bedrock milling elements, Molpa.

PLATE 5

"Rainrock" feature, Molpa.

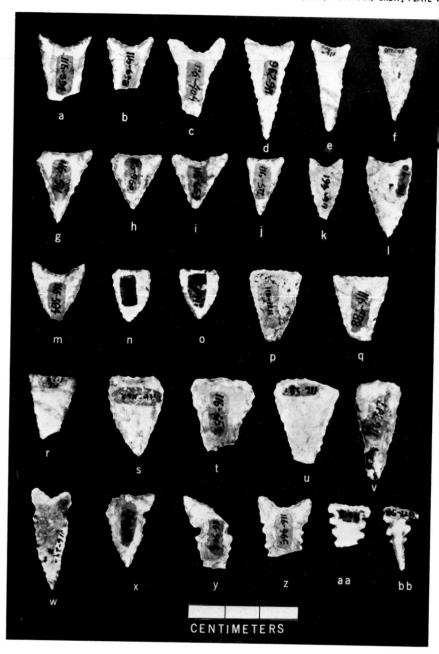

CENTIMETERS

PLATE 6

Projectile points and possible drill, Molpa.

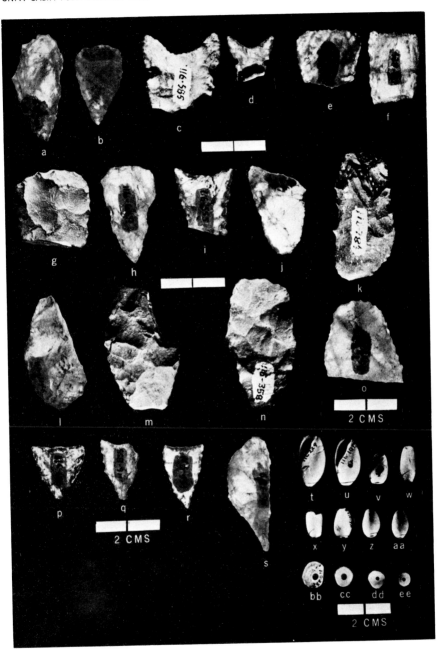

PLATE 7

Knives, drills and beads, Molpa.

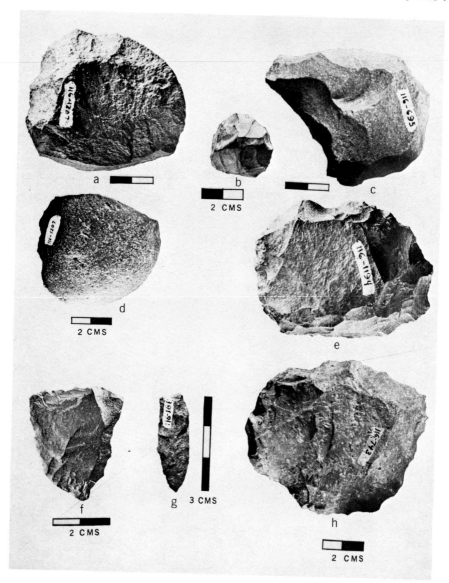

PLATE 8

Scrapers, knife, and wand insert, Molpa.

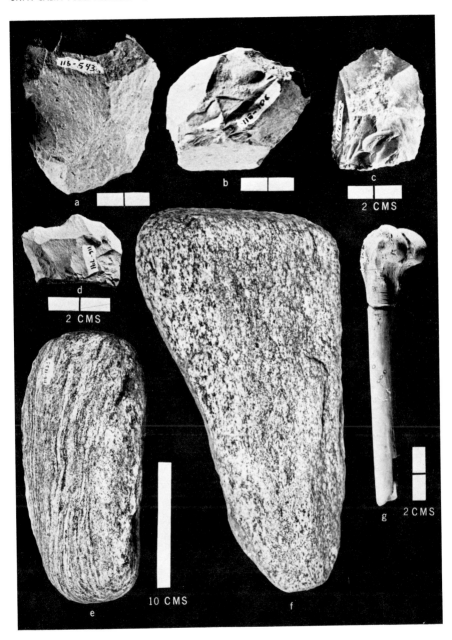

PLATE 9

Scrapers (planes), pestles, and incised bone, Molpa.

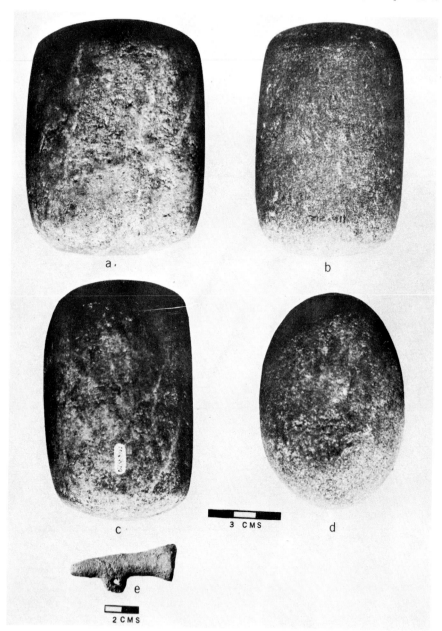

PLATE 10

Ceremonial pestles, mano, and miniature pipe, Molpa.

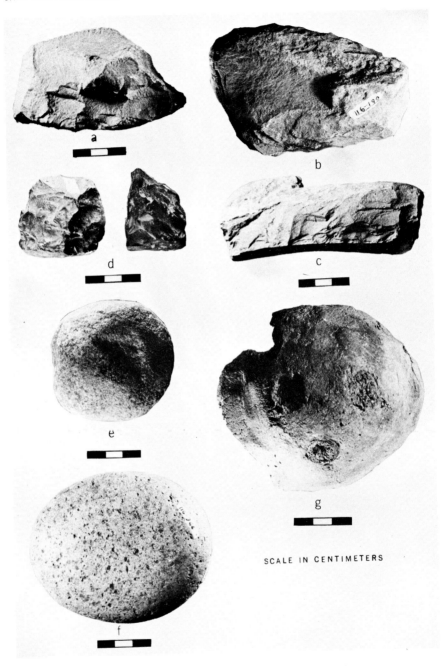

SCALE IN CENTIMETERS

PLATE 11

Scraper planes, scrapers, hammer, edge-ground cobble, and tripod pot, Molpa. Item C
is a sideview of scraper plane b.

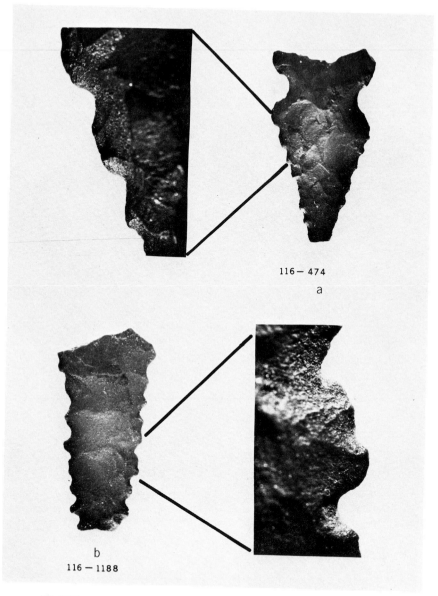

116 — 474

a

b

116 — 1188

PLATE 12

Serrated points and knives, showing wear on serrations.

3 CM

PLATE 13 APPENDIX B
Incised tablet (see appendix B).